SCIENCE FICTION GOLD

Cover: Changed to sea in an exquisite nightmare, painting by Jan Demila. WHEN WORLDS COLLIDE.

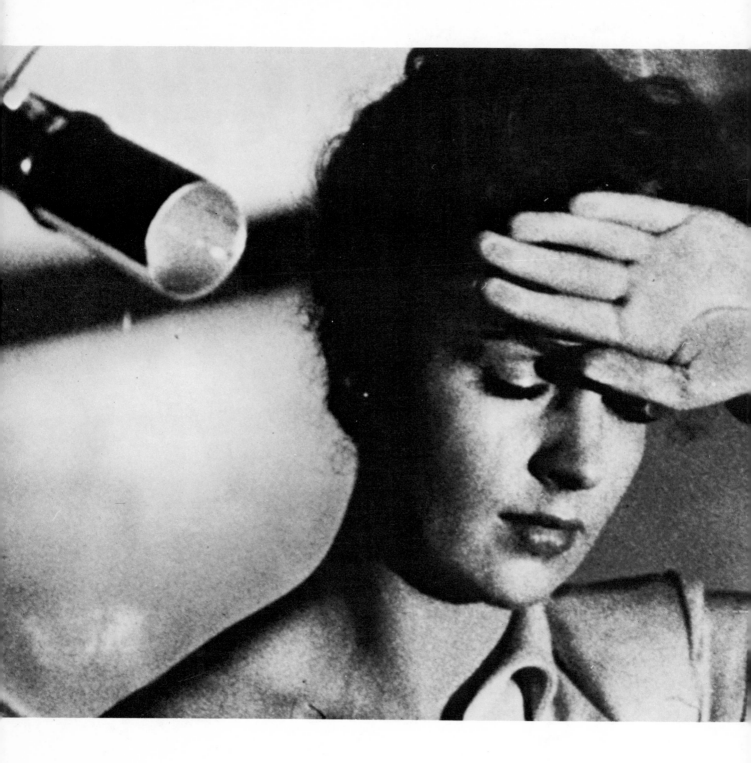

SCIENCE FICTION GOLD

FILM CLASSICS OF THE 50s

by DENNIS SALEH
FOREWORD by RAY HARRYHAUSEN

A Comma Book 🍃

McGraw-Hill Book Company

New York   St. Louis   San Francisco   Bogotá   Düsseldorf   Toronto
Mexico   Montreal   Panama   Paris   São Paulo   Tokyo   Madrid

Comma Books are designed, edited, and published by Dennis Saleh. This book published by McGraw-Hill Paperbacks, by arrangement with Comma Books, Inc.

1234567890HDHD 7832109

First Edition, 1979

ACKNOWLEDGMENTS

I wish to express my great thanks to the following for their help in making this book possible: Forrest J. Ackerman and the Ackerman Archives; Ray Harryhausen (for the introduction, background information, and the loan of a tentacle in the mail); George Pal; Scot Holton and Jeff Sillifant (for information, research materials, and photographs); Bob Wilkins, of CREATURE FEATURES, KTVU, Ch. 2, Oakland, California; science fiction film magazines: CINEFANTASTIQUE, FANTASCENE, FILMS FANTASTIQUE, PHOTON, SPFX (Special Effects). Two further research sources were of assistance: Walter Lee's REFERENCE GUIDE TO FANTASTIC FILMS (Chelsea-Lee Books, 1974, 3 vols.), and the Margaret Herrick Library of the Academy of Motion Picture Arts and Sciences.

The photographs in this book are part of the author's collection and were issued by the motion picture studios and production companies at the time of the films' original releases: Allied Artists, Columbia, Eagle-Lion, MGM, Paramount, RKO, 20th Century Fox, Universal, Warner Bros. Author photo: Judy Avery.

This book is dedicated to my Father, who took me to Palomar Observatory and to see INVADERS FROM MARS, and to Forry Ackerman, who in a better future will be everyone's uncle.

Library of Congress Cataloging in Publication Data

Saleh, Dennis, 1942-
    Science fiction gold.

    (Comma books)
    Filmography: p.
    1. Science fiction films — History and criticism.
2. Science fiction films — Catalogs.   I. Title.
PN1995.9.S26S2   791.43'0909'15   79-1257
ISBN 0-07-054467-0

CONTENTS

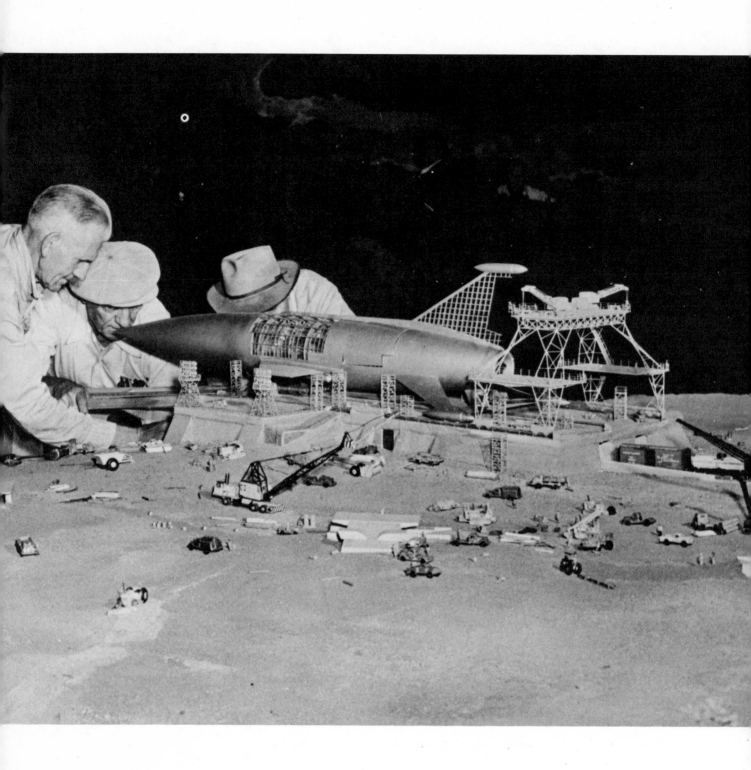

FOREWORD

Where does science fiction begin and fantasy leave off? Surely they must overlap. In fact, the term "science fiction," I should think, is really a subheading of the fantasy category. The fourteen films chosen for inclusion in this book all have one important thing in common — the stressing of the imaginative, the bizarre, the unusual point of view. The science fiction films of the 50s were inspired by films of the 30s which in turn owed their existence to the filmic gothic tales of the late 20s — earlier stimulated by the imaginative work of George Méliès. As Dennis Saleh so well points out in this book, the earlier cycles of this genre of film making were largely responsible for the present day science fiction successes, and were as well their basic inspiration.

Every work of art or scientific achievement must have a predecessor, something on which to build a fresh new idea. Hero worship is possibly another term for inspiration. My personal inspiration came mainly from the wonderful engravings of Victorian artist, Gustave Doré, the prehistoric animal paintings of Charles C. Knight, and the films of Willis O'Brien and Merian C. Cooper. The original KING KONG set off a spark in me that exploded into fifteen feature films and a number of animated short subjects. They were all largely sprinkled with bits and pieces of the original influences.

There is today a far larger audience for a well-made, so-called "science fiction" film than there was in the three earlier cycles of cinematic fantasy. One only has to look at the box office grosses for STAR WARS and SUPERMAN for verification. Science fiction film ideas were not always so easily sold to the motion picture studios and producers as they seem to be today. I once sold a story to producer Jack Dietz called "The Elementals," which could not get studio financing. My film, TWENTY MILLION MILES TO EARTH, was ignored for a long time before producer Charles Schneer had the wherewithal to raise money for its production.

And just after I finished making MIGHTY JOE YOUNG with Willis O'Brien, I drew a dozen charcoal sketches illustrating a possible stop-motion approach to an old H. G. Wells story called WAR OF THE WORLDS. It was a subject I had long wanted to put onto the motion picture screen. I even wrote to Orson Welles hoping his name and the memory of his dynamic radio broadcast of the same subject might aid in getting the project produced. A few years later George Pal was able to make the film for Paramount, with superb results. Eventually, there seems to be a time and place for every idea to come to fruition. Perhaps not quite the way one would imagine, but they do finally emerge into reality.

Preparations for the flight of the space Ark in WHEN WORLDS COLLIDE.

The unusual and detailed documentation and comments in SCIENCE FICTION GOLD will most certainly give future generations of film lovers a chance to understand and remember the origins of films of the future and to realize that there is "nothing new under the sun," only the way of doing it. For today's generations, perhaps the book will kindle a nostalgic reassessment of a genre of films which in their day might have appeared rather absurd to the large majority of an audience. I feel very fortunate indeed to have started my career and been a part of the growth of the "Cinema of the Imagination" during the 50s, and I am most pleased and proud that two of my films have been included in this homage to the science fiction films of the era — a decade of films that has been the direct inspiration for a new generation of film makers.

RAY HARRYHAUSEN

Not quite high noon in WAR OF THE WORLDS: plans for the Martian war ships.

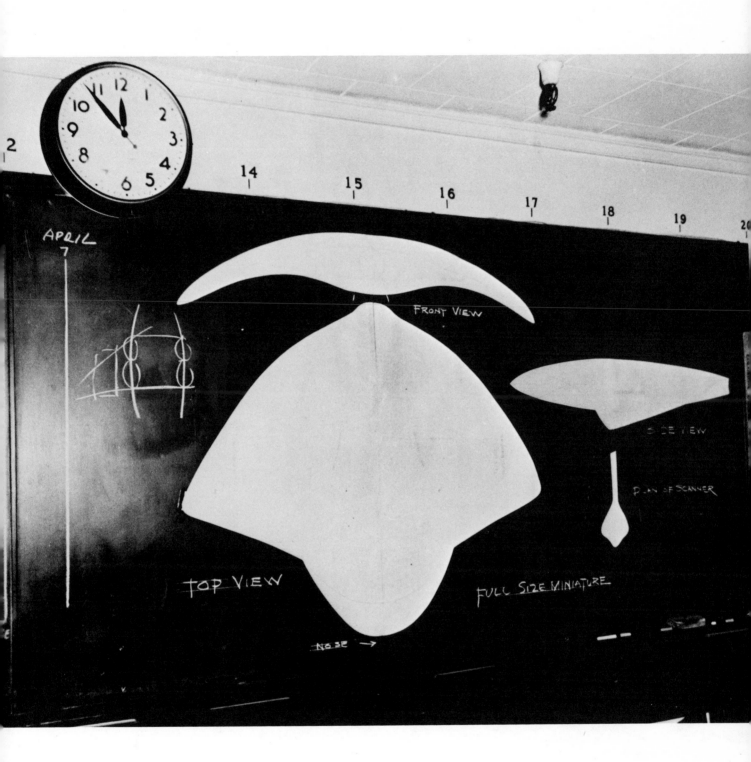

SCIENCE FICTION GOLD

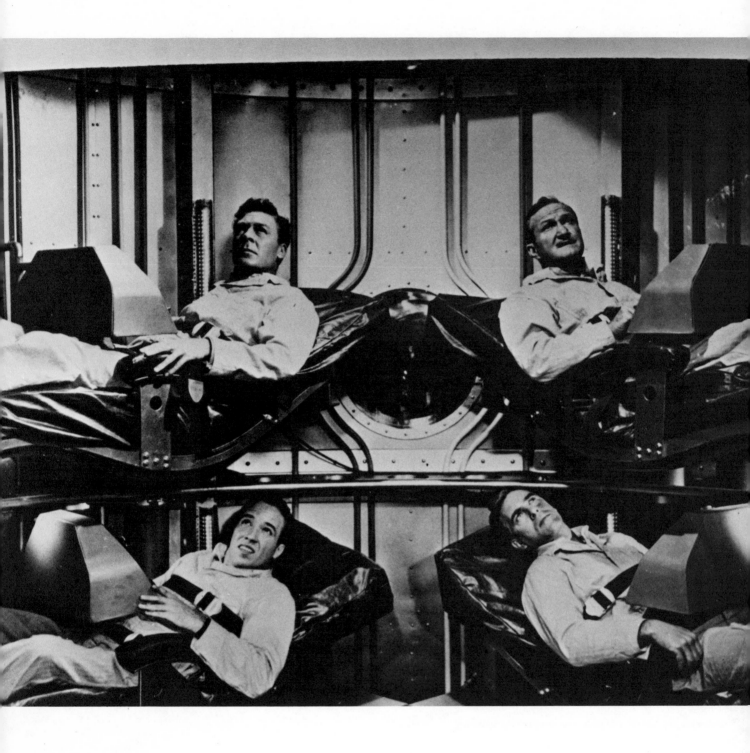

DESTINATION MOON

Where does the story of the future begin, but in the past. When the hatch clangs shut inside the spaceship LUNA, and it trembles and rises on the blast of its atomic engine, there are echoes reaching back to the dawning of rocketry in the Twentieth Century, and to the beginnings of science fiction film. DESTINATION MOON, begun in 1949 and completed and released in 1950, claims a pedigree dating from the 1920s, an ancestry of rocket inventors, European cinema, and political intrigue. The novel the movie was taken from, ROCKETSHIP GALILEO, by Robert A. Heinlein, was published in 1947, but to start at the beginning. . . .

In 1929, German movie director Fritz Lang, famed for METROPOLIS, the first classic science fiction epic, filmed the first authentic space travel movie, for UFA studio in Berlin. For DIE FRAU IM MOND (The Woman in the Moon), Lang enlisted Hermann Oberth and Willy Ley as technical advisors, both rocket enthusiasts and members of the historic German VfR, Society for Space Travel; this circle of experimenters set off explosions and fired cats in suitcases down rocket sled tracks on the outskirts of Berlin, and included young Wernher von Braun. Lang's film featured the first countdown in movies, acceleration shock, and weightlessness. Its rocket details were so good, Nazi authorities confiscated prints of the film in the 30s. Oberth and von Braun disappeared inside the German rocket effort. Ley left Germany for the U.S. and wrote about rockets. About the same time, another young man left Germany, ultimately for the U.S., George Pal, an animator from Hungary who worked at UFA in the early 30s.

Willy Ley came to special prominence during and after World War II with his authoritative books on rocketry and insider's details of the German rocket program. "Operation Paperclip," in the year following the war, brought von Braun and more than a hundred elite scientists to the U.S. By the end of the decade, the U.S. missile program was well into its own research with the V-2. In Hollywood, George Pal was a producer of animated short subjects using three-dimensional models. His fanciful PUPPETOONS series for Paramount studio won him a special achievement Oscar in 1944.

In 1949, Pal began his first two feature length movies, filmed back to back with the same production crew. The people who worked on THE GREAT RUPERT, starring Jimmy Durante and Rupert, an animated squirrel, also made the science fiction classic, DESTINATION

Inside the LUNA, the four men prepare for blast-off.

MOON. Technical advisors for the space production were author Heinlein, and noted astronomical artist, Chesley Bonestell, co-author of one of the two Willy Ley books considered texts on the set, and a veteran Hollywood set artist.

Heinlein's novel even had distinct echoes of the past that were finally eliminated from the movie script. In ROCKETSHIP GALILEO, a scientist, Dr. Cargraves, and three high school boys build an atomic rocket and make what they think is the first journey to the Moon. There they discover Nazis, a complete rocket base, and plans for bombarding the Earth with atomic missiles. The ambiguous threatening powers in DESTINATION MOON are clearly not Nazis, but the danger is the same. The movie begins with an abortive rocket launch, and immediate talk of sabotage. When a group of U.S. industrialists meets to discuss a rocket effort, they are told in no uncertain terms: "We're not the only ones who know the Moon can be reached. The race is on. The first country that can use the Moon for the launching of missiles will control the Earth. That, gentlemen, is the most important military fact of this century."

Though only a minor element in the movie, the sabotage and intrigue of a space race added unmistakable and timely drama. Russian expansion in Eastern Europe following World War II had left the country uneasy; the announcement in 1949 that the Soviets had atom bombs only confirmed the public's fears. Worse, 1950 brought disclosures that the Soviets had been funneled secret U.S. atomic data from 1942 to 1949, by a physicist who had worked at the government research facility in Los Alamos, New Mexico, birthplace of the atomic bomb.

The threat of the moonbase, and the novel's taste of authenticity, are about all of ROCKETSHIP GALILEO that reach the screen. The three boys become a General Thayer, "a satellite rocket man who crusaded himself out of the service," Jim Barnes, an industrialist, and Joe Sweeney, a hapless radio technician near-shanghaied aboard the LUNA. Pal intentionally cast the film with non-star leads — Warner Anderson, Tom Powers, John Archer, Dick Wesson, a practice common to his first sci-fi films. He preferred unknown players whose lack of familiarity would help lend a story credibility. This "no stars" look was characteristic of most of the sci-fi movies of the 50s; few name actors appeared in any of them.

The story of DESTINATION MOON is essentially how Cargraves, Thayer, and Barnes join forces to build and fly a ship to the Moon. After Cargraves' failure in the first minutes of the film, Thayer meets with Barnes in the next scene, two years later, at Barnes Aircraft Corporation. He says Army intelligence "knows" the rocket was blown up, and argues that although the government is unwilling to pursue space research in peacetime, they will

Cargraves, alone at the tail of the ship, floats free.

need it soon enough. He enlists Barnes' support, who assembles the country's leading industrialists for a crash course on rocketry — using a Walter Lantz Woody Woodpecker cartoon — and to hear Thayer's proposal. In a few fast moments, Woody Woodpecker and the General's remark about a moonbase marshal the industrialists' money and determination. A montage of technological images follows — draftsmen, spaceship designs, a model rocket, leading to the LUNA itself, at its desert site, Dry Wells Airfield.

The rich confusion of a construction site and scaffoldings leads the eye up past cranes and gantries to the rocket, stark and skeletal in its beginnings. A full-size mock-up of the LUNA's tail fins and bottom loomed up at the location site in Apple Valley, northeast of San Bernardino, California, in the Mojave Desert. Like DIE FRAU IM MOND, two decades earlier, DESTINATION MOON was to be a realistic, even semi-documentary depiction of the possibilities of space travel, and night filming with the mock-up at the desert setting was just part of the monumental efforts that went into production.

The special effects crew performed wonders of design and engineering, under the direction of Lee Zavitz, known in Hollywood as the man who burned Atlanta in GONE WITH THE WIND. Pal's animators provided the second LUNA, a miniature from Bonestell and Heinlein's rocket design, nearly four feet tall. A growing body of scientists and engineers visited the movie sets, including the esteemed Willy Ley, sparking the enthusiasm for authenticity. Statistics for an actual flight were plotted, and precise orbits for the Earth and Moon calculated by Dr. Robert Richardson of Mount Wilson Observatory, above nearby Pasadena. The result of the prodigious effort was another Pal Oscar, for the movie's special effects.

Take-off comes abruptly in the film. Intrigue surrounding the rocket is on the increase: permission to test the atomic engine at the site is denied; a newspaper headline heralds, "Mass Meeting Protest Radioactive Rocket." Barnes speculates that the outcry is orchestrated, and that someone is out to stop them. He says they must go immediately — leave in seventeen hours, with an impromptu crew of himself, Cargraves, and Thayer; Sweeney is enlisted because the original radio man is in the hospital. His fearful gulps and bewilderment provide comic relief in the film; Sweeney is a figure the audience identifies with, an ordinary soul among the scientists. The hours run out as a jeep roars up to the base gate; a shouting man insists he has a court order forbidding the launch. (The court order in Heinlein's original story forbade Cargraves' taking three minors to the Moon!) It is 3:50 A.M. and too late, as the ship's engine fires and takes hold, and we see the LUNA lift off in the ship's viewing screen.

Inside the cabin, the men are crushed into their acceleration couches (air cushions

Barnes rides the tank out to Cargraves, rescuing him.

that deflated and inflated on cue through a compressed air system). Their faces smear and distend in the grimace of monstrous gravitational pull (a gauze membrane fitted on each actor's face, and then stretched by off-camera attachments). Soon the men experience "free orbit," weightlessness, and begin to float about the cabin. Barnes dons magnetic shoes and passes them to the others, in a delightful and convincing space ballet, air walking to the reassuring clink of his boots on the walls.

The floating effect took the construction of a marvel of set design. The cabin room was suspended in an enormous three-story steel rig patterned after a cement mixer, so it could be turned at any angle. For a particular shot, the entire cabin would be rotated to the desired position, and the men dropped in from overhead wires. Each cabin wall panel was removable, to allow the actors and camera in at different angles. The camera and lights — mounted on a special giant boom — were actually "built-in" parts of the set. The operation was so elaborate and so expensive, epic master Cecil B. DeMille visited the set to satisfy his curiosity.

Working with the actors on wires continued in the dramatic space rescue. When the men discover a radar antenna will not extend, they have to go outside and free it. Thayer stays behind in the ship, as the three set out in spacesuits, fitted inside with iron harnesses to attach the overhead wires. Like over-sized puppets, the men dangled from frames worked by a crew of "puppeteers," sometimes hanging in the air for two hours for a few seconds of filmed action. There was great concern with the effectiveness of the wire work and the illusion of weightlessness. A crewman would spend entire days daubing reflections on the wires with black paint. When the men prepare to go outside the ship, they are in "free orbit," and wearing their magnetic boots. During one take, the locker they open contained hanging — and not floating — spacesuits. The suits were immediately wired to float, and the scene reshot.

Occasionally, a camera would simply shoot footage turned upsidedown, as when the men first appear outside the ship and hang in space. The three are motionless a moment in the enormity of space, and the Moon beside them is like a fourth gleaming helmet. They set off around the ship, walking upside down. Then Cargraves, alone at the tail of the ship, kneels to examine something, and for a moment floats free. He realizes too late what is happening and is loose, floating away from the LUNA. Barnes radios Thayer to bring an oxygen tank, concocting an ingenious rescue.

Barnes rides the tank out to Cargraves, using the blast of the nozzle as a miniature rocket, and brings him back to the ship. The oxygen tank, a balsa wood mock-up fitted with a CO_2 cartridge, further complicated things. When the carbon dioxide discharge began to

The ship turns in space braking its descent.

fall — and not float, footage for the sequence had to be edited together from short pieces of film before the discharge began to fall. To help provide distance perspective in cramped soundstage quarters, a midget actor in a midget spacesuit was used in shots of the rescue and on the lunar surface.

Take-off, flight, and landing of the ship were made up of footage combining live action with the full-size mock-up and animation photography using the miniature LUNA. This animation work was essentially stop-motion photography: photographing an object, slightly changing its posture and position, and rephotographing it, to provide "moving" footage. The stunning long shot of the LUNA and the three spacemen walking on its side was animation photography of tiny model spacemen. This painstaking work took up to 24 different position set-ups for a second of film. The eighty minutes of live action took less time to shoot than five minutes of animation. Pal's animators produced delights like tiny floodlights at the rocket site the size of thimbles, that worked, bathing the miniature LUNA in poured light.

When the Moon fills the viewing screen, the ship turns in space and fires its engine, braking its descent. As Sweeney radios Washington, D.C., Cargraves and Barnes prepare to set foot on the surface. The door to the airlock swings open, and the camera pans slowly across the craggy, white landscape, to the Earth hanging in the sky above a mountainous ridge. Cargraves steps off the ladder and says, "By the grace of God and in the name of the United States of America, I take possession of this planet in behalf of and for the benefit of all mankind." Heinlein and Bonestell debated literal features of the Moon's surface, picking a landing spot. Bonestell prevailed with Crater Harpalus, where the Earth would be visible low in the sky, above the crater's rim. The landscape set was an elaborate arrangement of models, paintings by Bonestell, photographs of the paintings, blowups, and black velvet backdrops, used in various combinations for different perspectives and camera angles.

Lighting the lunar surface and outer space proved a challenge. To produce the starry sky, 2000 automobile headlight bulbs were used, fitted into a network of 70,000 feet of wire. Because the lights produced red halos on color film, each had to be covered with a gelatin screen, that melted and had to be replaced twice a day. The intense brilliance of light needed for the Moon's surface took hanging arc lights, massed in numbers to the safety limit. Different colored spacesuits provided identification at distances, and the added attraction of highlights in the stark, black and white settings used in this first color science fiction film.

The men set up equipment, detect possible traces of uranium, and engage in horseplay.

The landscape of the Crater Harpalus and the LUNA.

The last struggle comes when new fuel calculations put the ship over take-off weight. They strip the ship of gear, and eighteen minutes away from departure time — determined by the optimal distance of the Earth in its orbit — they are still 110 pounds overweight. For a moment, an uneasy realization creeps across the men's faces. Then Sweeney tricks the others and leaves the ship, radioing them to leave him behind. Barnes, staring out the viewer at him in his spacesuit, devises another rescue, and talks Sweeney back on board. They tear out the radio and throw it overboard, then drop Sweeney's spacesuit and an oxygen tank, using holes drilled in the airlock and lines hanging outside the ship — more than enough weight.

The ship blasts into space and the Earth grows in the sky, as the LUNA races homeward. Then we see the words, "This is the end," followed by, "of the Beginning." Indeed, Pal's $586,000 production proved a smash success at the box office and set off the explosion of science fiction films in the early 50s. The authenticity of the film stirred great response, though still considered wild imagination by many. Who could guess the immediate prophecy of DESTINATION MOON: not just the eventual Moon landing two decades later, but the step into outer space in just seven years, the orbiting of the Russian Sputnik. As the movie said, it was time for the skies. And there was another, altogether different reason why the skies lit with fascination for Americans, an idea not explored in DESTINATION MOON, the possibility that interplanetary space travel was not a one-way street.

Stripped of gear, the ship is still over take-off weight.

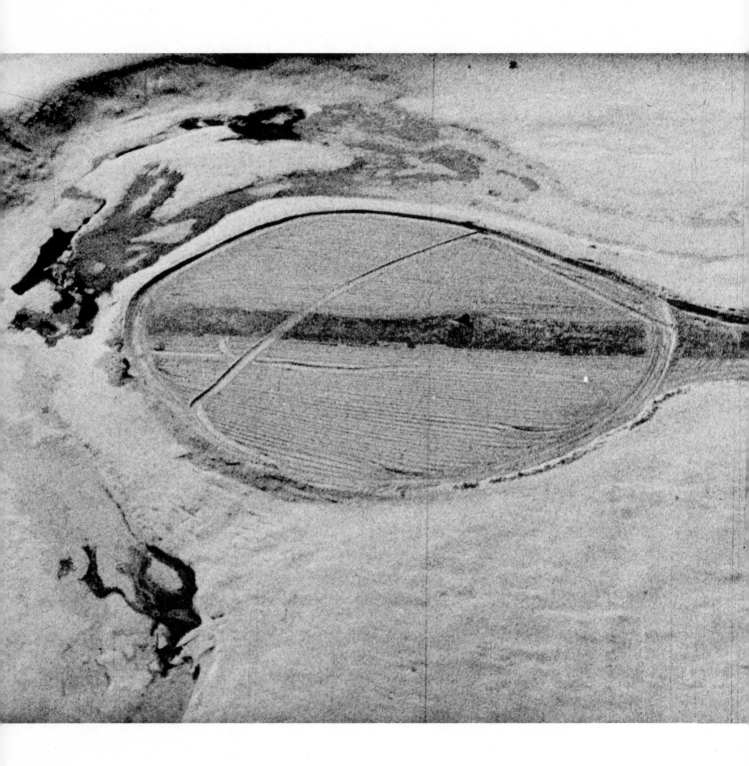

THE THING

White, white. The blast of the launching rocket, the glaring tip of ignition and white heat. The Moon, white in the sky, a light in the window showing the future the way here. White arcs of electricity, white snapping lines rising in the doctor's laboratory. Then snow, white of the polar regions; in the Shelley novel, Frankenstein's monster trudging into the blank expanse and distance. White, the snows of Mars. White, like the future of the colors. With white, something is always about to happen. It pushes things forward; it makes things overly apparent, nightmarishly real. White italicizes the air with its starkness, it makes everything ready. White blips on a radar screen, photographs of white objects floating in the sky, glowing white lights.

1951, high noon in the heyday of the 50s saucer bender, when the first great flying saucer movies came to town. Beginning in the summer of 1947, the U.S. experienced increasing waves of flying saucer sightings, lasting well into the 50s. In June of 1947 a businessman flying near Mt. Rainier, Washington, reported seeing nine objects flying in a formation, "like a saucer would if you skipped it across the water." Within 24 hours, the expression "flying saucer" was loose in the land, out of the newspapers and on every tongue. Within a month, there were sightings in every state in the country. Saucers were seen over Muroc Air Force Base in California. In the famous Gorman chase, an Air Force pilot tried to catch a saucer over Fargo, North Dakota. Over Fort Knox, Kentucky, Air National Guard Captain Thomas Mantell crashed and died chasing a saucer, after radioing that the craft was "tremendous in size" and "metallic." Radio personality Arthur Godfrey said he was buzzed by a saucer while piloting a plane. Popular uproar grew with each year; along with radioactivity and communism, flying saucers were a pet raw nerve with the public.

1949 brought the inevitable first flying saucer movie, called simply that, THE FLYING SAUCER. A minor effort, filmed independently of the Hollywood studios, it never surfaced nationally. The film was saved from total obscurity in the mid-70s, when a film distributor rebuilt the last, disintegrating print. THE FLYING SAUCER was like a fast read of the nation's headlines: an agent is dispatched to investigate saucer sightings and discovers both an alien craft and lurking Russians. But Russians in the film made a kind of geographical sense, considering their proximity to the Aleutian Islands. The underground

Like the head of a sperm and its tail, a buried seed.

movie was set in Alaska, anticipating producer Howard Hawks' masterpiece of two years later, THE THING.

As the credits begin, snow and wind trail in the background, the licking tongue of the polar north. We see the title burned, or torn, into the screen letter by letter: "T-H-E T-H-I-N-G" — total, entire, complete ambiguity, content-free, like a white word. It was the most ambitious and most successful of the "It" titles. Prior to the movie's release, a series of mysterious advertisements appeared in a variety of science fiction, mystery, and western pulp magazines, proclaiming "You can't kill THE THING with a gun." Or asking starkly, "What is THE THING?"

As drifts of snow whip up, a lone figure approaches the officers club at an Air Force base in Anchorage, Alaska. It is Ned Scott, a reporter newly arrived at the base, looking for a story. In a short time, Scott is in a plane with Captain Pat Hendry, bound for a research base 2000 miles to the north, where a party of scientists reported a mysterious crash. There is speculation: "Could be Russians. They're all over the pole like flies." As the plane banks we see the base below, perched precariously at the edge of nature, a few dark rises in limitless white stretches. Throughout the film, the inhospitable elements will never be far from hand, heightening the tension of the life-and-death struggle. All the while the small party faces the terror stalking them, the snow and wind press in.

The next morning, Hendry sees the leader of the expedition, Dr. Carrington, about the crash. The scientist's notes relate an enormous explosion recorded on a seismograph. Photos were taken by cameras triggered by radioactivity; the white blips suggest a falling meteor, but in one photo the "meteor" is seen rising. A group flies to the location of the disturbance, and from overhead makes out a buried form. For a moment, there is a glint of reflection in the middle of the area, from something rising above the snow. The dark, obscured mass and the strange skid marks leading to it look like the head of a sperm and its tail, a buried seed.

When the men land, they find the object at the center of the shape is some kind of stabilizer, like an airplane fin; the Geiger counters come wildly to life. Carrington suggests they spread out to determine the size and shape of their find. The men step back from each other, stretching their arms, until the mounting background music abruptly stops, and we are jarred along with the men at their realization: "It's almost a perfect —" "It is. It's round." "We finally got one. We found a flying saucer."

When they attempt to melt the covering ice with a thermite bomb, they set off explosions that destroy the craft. Then, some distance from the blow-up, another form

"It's round." "We finally got one. We found a flying saucer."

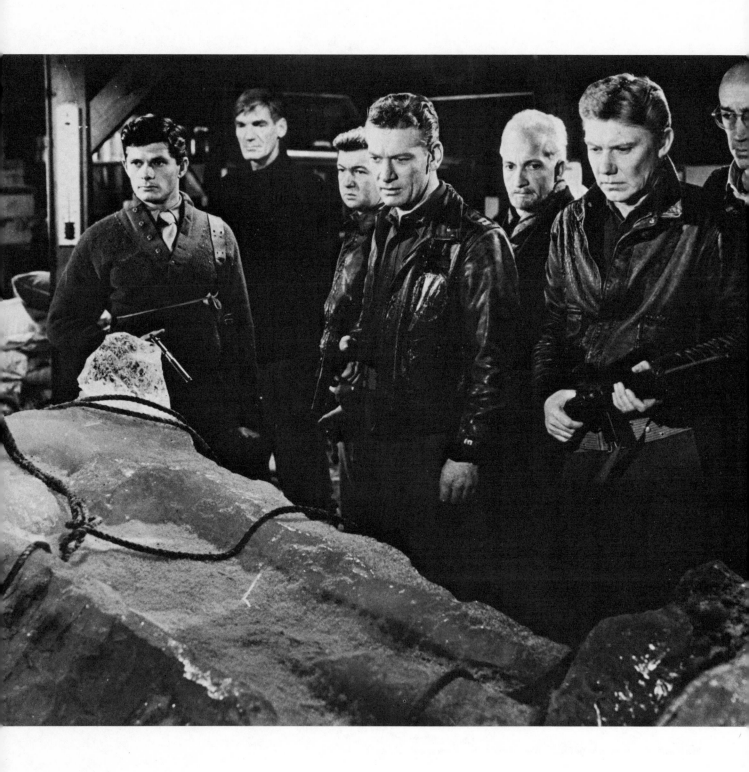

is found frozen beneath the ice, over eight feet long, with legs, a head, the pilot of the saucer thrown free in the explosion, the "Thing." Hendry directs the men to chop the creature free in a block of ice, and takes unmistakable command of the situation, as the presence of the Thing now begins to unsettle matters: Already, he's had to block Scott from radioing his story to the world: "I'm not working for the world. I'm working for the Air Force."

Kenneth Tobey as Hendry and Douglas Spencer as Scott — Scotty — give definitive performances in their roles as two favorite sci-fi film characters, the reporter and the military commander. The reporter gets to prod, to ask questions; he gets us information. At the start of the film, Scotty recalls Carrington was at Bikini, site of two U.S. A-bomb tests in the South Pacific in 1946. Spencer steals about half the scenes he's in, tall, standing over most of the cast, looking in the way of even his own overcoat. He's the first to attack the ice with an axe, in his excitement over their find; later he stands ready to meet the Thing in a darkened walkway, with a butcher cleaver in his hand. At the end of the film, he's given its best known lines to intone, the clarion call about visitors from outer space.

Tobey gives more than the journeyman-adequate acting job so often found in science fiction films. He is exemplary in the no-nonsense, let's-deal-with-it school of action. He banters good-naturedly throughout the film with Scotty; he holds off the driven entreaties of Carrington; he deals with the Thing. He even carries off an intrigue with Nikki, Carrington's secretary (Margaret Sheridan). A funny and odd little scene occurs during a few spare moments the first night at the camp. Nikki is seen pouring a cocktail into Hendry's mouth, while he sits with his hands tied behind him. They tease and flirt about a previous encounter, and she finally kisses him. This scene is now gone in most prints of THE THING. After the film's original release, some footage was edited out, notably the kissing scene. THE THING was so successful it was released three times — in 1951, 1954, and 1957.

THE THING, unlike most sci-fi movies, is an actors' film, with its emphasis on the suspense of the unseen and the rapid interaction of the characters. There are little or no special effects, besides a bit of asbestos suit work for a stuntman and a vivid display of electricity. Pace carries the movie, the continuing collisions of the men, and performances like Tobey's. There should be some kind of honorary society or club for the actors and actresses who starred in these films, and you could call it the Kenneth Tobey Club, in honor of his selfless performances in a number of sci-fi films. These players turned in no-frills, no-tantrums acting jobs, agreed to act first of all as if they believed in the stories, and to step aside unhesitatingly for some piece of exotic hardware or preposterous monster.

Hendry and the others find the shape of the creature in the melted ice.

"Name" stars were the exception in these films, and few of the genre's principals went beyond science fiction roles in movies. Some of the era's players did resurface on television, however, like James Arness who played the Thing, and later became TV's long-reigning Marshal Matt Dillon on GUNSMOKE. If one looks closely at certain sci-fi movies, there are familiar faces from TV series stretching over three decades, from FATHER KNOWS BEST to HAWAII 5-0 and THE SIX MILLION DOLLAR MAN. If you look closely in THE THING, you'll also see the announcer/straight man from Groucho Marx's long-running 50s TV quiz show, YOU BET YOUR LIFE — George Fennemen playing one of the scientists.

Robert Cornthwaite is also exemplary as the third lead, Carrington, an archetypal science fiction scientist, down to his distinguished, no, engraved gray hair, and goatee. The encounter between the scientist and the military leader is classic: the primitive, survival brain of the soldier versus the advanced, frontal lobe brain of the scientist. Carrington wants to begin thawing out the creature immediately in order to study it, but Hendry insists on waiting for orders. The block is left in a storeroom open to the freezing temperatures. An electric blanket is mistakenly thrown over the ice because one of the men can't stand seeing its eyes peering up, and the Thing unfreezes. Hendry and the others find the melted block and the shape of the creature in the slab. After the Thing makes good its escape, the men retrieve its forearm and hand, torn off fighting with dogs.

Scientists and Air Force men alike crowd around a table, where the limb is bathed in light. The evidence of the hand is incredible, but the scientists suggest the visitor is a form of vegetative life. Scotty gets the scene's best line, "An intellectual carrot." Carrington answers him: "This carrot, as you call it, has constructed an aircraft capable of flying millions of miles through space, propelled by a force unknown by us." He postulates on evolution of plants rather than animals on another planet, and says they must communicate with the Thing. As the search for the creature begins, Carrington enlists the scientists in a conspiracy to deal with the Thing without Hendry's knowledge. He posts his own guards in a greenhouse, when he finds evidence the Thing has been there — a blood-drained, shrunken dog corpse.

The next day, we hear that two of the scientists are hanging from the greenhouse beams upside down, throats torn open. The nature of the threat is finally clear: the Thing is a vampire. Carrington informs the scientists the Thing sought out the greenhouse, the only soil for hundreds of miles around, for a purpose. During the night, Carrington experimented with seeds taken from under the fingernails of the creature's hand. He saturated soil with plasma taken from the camp's blood bank, and in a few short hours had a small bed of "Things." The scientists are aghast at the growth of the sprouts and their

The scientists are aghast at the growth of the sprouts.

sounds, pulsing like tiny bellows: "Almost like the wail of a newborn child that's hungry."

For all the movie's contemporary trappings, there is a wealth of standard elements from the horror movies of the 30s and 40s, including the scientist who tinkers with the creation of life. As originally shot, the film had even greater horror impact, including a good deal more footage of the Thing. Final editing eliminated such positively horrific doings as the Thing seen hanging the two men in the beams, and biting one in the throat. Sensibly, some things are left to the audience's imagination. Our few glimpses of the Thing are fleeting, obscured, often in shadow. What is suggested becomes as important as what is seen.

The movie is a good deal more restrained, even, than the original story it was based on, "Who Goes There?" by John W. Campbell, Jr., famed editor of ASTOUNDING magazine in the 40s and 50s. Campbell's monster has tentacles, blue worm hair, three red eyes, and fangs. It has protoplasm that makes it a kind of monstrous chameleon, becoming anything alive it comes into contact with. Men in Campbell's South Pole base see a Thing that is half-alien protoplasm, and half-dead dog. It becomes fourteen of the men before it is stopped. Some advertising for the film used these concepts in an artwork combination of tentacles and "protoplasmic" lettering for the title. However much the film was originally toned down, it suffered additional editing upon its release in England. There, the censors snipped out some footage of the Thing's last scene, and issued the movie an "X," Adults Only, rating.

The first actual encounter with the Thing is a shocker. Hendry throws open the greenhouse door to find it standing confronting them, forearm grown back and all. In the film's only close-ups of the creature's face, we make out its humanoid appearance. In a few, fast glimpses, we see exaggerated slashes of makeup, peculiar angular eyebrows, jagged features. It has a high, domed, bald head, and wears an ambiguous uniform-like garment. Arness as the Thing looms over the men, with four inches of boot heels added to his six feet five inches of height. The Thing's howl and roar, as he struggles in the doorway, is the yowl of a cat slowed down and amplified. Design concepts for the Thing went through more than a dozen sculpted renditions. The final result is like nothing so much as a cross between the original Boris Karloff Frankenstein monster and one of the bizarre backdrops in the first classic horror film, CABINET OF DR. CALIGARI.

Now the film moves quickly to its climax. Nikki offhandedly gives the men a clue about what to do with a vegetable, "Boil it. Boil it, stew it, bake it, fry it." Then the Thing attacks again and is fought off doused in gasoline, and set on fire; it throws itself out a window and runs off into the snows. The final confrontation comes when the Thing destroys the camp's

The survival brain of the soldier versus the frontal lobe brain of the scientist.

heating system, and the party makes a stand at the electrical generator. In the dimness of one of the corridor walkways, a trap is laid using three electrical lines. The party is plunged into darkness. Throughout the film, we have gone back and forth between the lighted rooms of the base and the narrow, dimly-lit corridors that connect the rooms, unheated walkways like tunnels. In the dark it is hard to tell one bundled figure from another. The dialogue overlaps more and more, making it difficult to tell who is speaking; this realistic touch is present everywhere in the movie, but nowhere more effectively. As the men peer to make out the advance of the Thing, there is confusion among themselves.

Carrington raves at Hendry in the walkway: "Knowledge is more important than life, Captain. It doesn't matter what happens to us, nothing counts except our thinking. We owe it to the species of our brain to stand here and die without destroying a source of wisdom. Civilization has given us order." When the creature appears, Carrington shuts off the generator. He rushes forward pleading for communication but is struck aside by the Thing as the electricity hits it. The remarkable sequence of the Thing shrinking as it is electrocuted was photographed using successively smaller actors in Thing makeup, and a small model set afire. First the right arc snaps out to the creature, then the left and overhead bolts. The Thing drops to its knees. The electricity fires down relentlessly, until the snaps beat at a pile of disintegrating ashes, wisps of a vampire caught in the dawn light, stuffing of a scarecrow, nothing.

At the film's conclusion, Scotty is at last able to get his story out. The intermittent storms have cleared to allow transmission, and Hendry says there's no further reason to wait. In the background, Nikki teases Hendry about marriage and the size of a captain's salary. We hear that Carrington suffered only a broken collarbone. It is mopping up time, but not before Scotty ends the movie with the fateful warning: "North Pole, November third, Ned Scott reporting. One of the world's greatest battles was fought and won today by the human race. Here, at the top of the world, a handful of American soldiers and civilians met the first invasion from another planet. A man by the name of Noah once saved our world with an ark of wood. Here at the North Pole a few men performed a similar service with an arc of electricity. The flying saucer which landed here, and its pilot, have been destroyed. And now, before giving you the details of the battle, I bring you a warning. Every one of you listening to my voice, tell the world, tell this to everybody wherever they are. Watch the skies, everywhere, keep looking, keep watching the skies."

The arcs of electricity beat down relentlessly on the Thing.

THE DAY THE EARTH STOOD STILL

Radar, science fiction's faithful watch. Through the years, it has stood vigil in the greatest and least of sci-fi films. A group of small buildings lies together; like dogs, they raise the ears of the radar, the great mechanical bat ears. Then the turning cups pressed to the sky are like a detective listening into the apartment next door; there is a mystery. Hong Kong, Calcutta, France, England, radar is tracking something moving across the face of the planet, "a large unidentified object circling the Earth at incredible speeds," radios the BBC. When it is reported over the U.S., it is traveling 4000 miles an hour.

So begins THE DAY THE EARTH STOOD STILL, the second great flying saucer movie released in 1951. By the time Klaatu parked his saucer in Washington, D.C., across Pennsylvania Avenue from the White House, there had been hundreds of saucer sightings. In the furor surrounding the Mantell crash, the government commissioned the Air Force's "Project Blue Book," to tally and scrutinize sightings. The country became familiar with the names of flying saucer experts, like Edward J. Ruppelt, first director of "Bluebook," who coined the term, "UFO." Flying saucer groups sprang up, saucer magazines, people were beginning to claim contact with the saucers, and their inhabitants. At White Sands Missile Range, in New Mexico, site of the fledgling U.S. space program, a technician reported being whisked aboard a saucer and flown to New York and back in half an hour.

Saucer interest peaked dramatically in this country in the early 50s, but the sightings here and elsewhere were by no means unique to the era. During World War II, Allied fliers over Germany reported being tagged by strange, glowing balls, "Foo Fighters," they were called, at first thought to be new German weaponry. In the 1870s, saucers were sighted throughout Europe and the world. In 1883 the first photographs of saucers were taken, by a Professor Bonilla at an observatory in Zacatecas, Mexico. In 1897, an enormous "airship" was seen by a farmer in Kansas, as well as others in several states.

Inveterate saucerologists have traced sightings back through history to antiquity. The Roman historian Livy wrote of an object in the sky that looked like a flying shield. Egyptian papyruses contain saucer references, as do the Hindu Vedas. Even the Bible has been used as a saucer text. In the most familiar passage, the prophet Ezekiel describes creatures in the land of the Chaldeans: "The appearance of the wheels and their work

Klaatu's saucer parked in Washington, D.C.

was like unto the colour of a beryl: and they four had one likeness: and their appearance and their work was as it were a wheel in the middle of a wheel . . . And when the living creatures went, the wheels went by them: and when the living creatures were lifted from the earth, the wheels were lifted up."

Ezekiel regarded the fiery, glowing creatures and wheels as signs from God. Angels, cherubim, they were emissaries from the heavens. In THE DAY THE EARTH STOOD STILL, Klaatu comes on a mission from the skies, in a great glowing wheel of a saucer. He represents transcendent power and has come to offer mankind salvation from holocaust. His stature in the film and his fate suggest the figure of Christ and a science fiction version of the Ascension. Klaatu comes to Earth and goes among the people. Like Romans, soldiers first wound and then kill Klaatu. His robot, Gort, melts a wall as if rolling away a stone, and Klaatu arisen gives man one last chance, before returning to the skies.

In the story the movie was taken from, author Harry Bates' (founding editor of ASTOUNDING magazine in the 30s) description of Klaatu makes him into a heavenly figure: "Out stepped a man, godlike in appearance and human in form. The first thing he did was to raise his right arm high in the universal gesture of peace; but it was not that which impressed those nearest so much as the expression on his face, which radiated kindness, wisdom, the purest nobility. In his delicately tinted robe he looked like a benign god."

Bates' story did not provide much of the film's screenplay, though. In "Farewell to the Master," set in the capital in an unspecified future time, a saucer lands and Klaatu and a robot, Gnut, appear. A madman shoots and kills Klaatu, and Gnut becomes immobile. A photographer later hides at the saucer, because he has photos showing the robot's feet moved. The photographer and the robot interact finally. At one point, Gnut carries the man in his arms, clearly the inspiration for the movie robot, Gort's taking actress Patricia Neal in his arms. There's also a useless "glasstex" cube Gnut is sealed in, like the Army's experimental KL 93 plastic that Gort melts in DAY. Gnut doesn't have equipment as good as Gort's, and only reproduces hologram-like images of Klaatu, not the living, breathing model in the movie. In an encounter with a tank, Gnut is much more direct than Gort with his fantastic ray. Gnut actually runs to the tank and strikes it, smashing the cannon. At the end of the story, Gnut reveals the twist, that he, the robot, and not Klaatu, was the master.

Action in DAY THE EARTH STOOD STILL begins with the saucer landing, glowing and humming down through the skies over Washington. Two weeks location shooting provided background footage throughout the movie. Newsman Drew Pearson begins a radio

The crowd and military see Gort appear on the ramp.

and TV broadcast about the landing, a special touch of realism and first for sci-fi films. Pearson also filmed a special advertising trailer about the movie, using his familiar radio format. Other real life news personalities included in the film were H. V. Kaltenborn and Gabriel Heater. A mass of people is cordoned off by lines of police. The ship landed at 3:47 EST and is now surrounded by soldiers, tanks, and artillery, the unmistakable military flexing so necessary and common in sci-fi films in the 50s, as though the rattling of movie sabers were a fantasy release for international jitters. In parts of the movie, Washington looks like an armed camp, rife with jeeps and trucks full of soldiers careening in the night. This is no outpost cut off from civilization, but that other preferred target in most sci-fi, one of the great metropolises, the Nation's Capital.

The silver white craft was a full-size, 350-foot diameter mock-up, 25-feet high, built on a 20th Century Fox back lot. Though publicity notes said the ship cost $100,000, it was mostly plaster of paris over a framework; the only solid part was the ramp. The invisible entrance to the saucer was manually opened and closed by workmen hidden inside each time it was used. Special effects were under the direction of Fred Sersen, a previous Oscar winner for his work. As Pearson's voice continues over the scene, the saucer suddenly projects out the odd platform, and opens. Klaatu (Michael Rennie) walks down the ramp and onto the lawn, proclaiming, "We have come to visit you in peace and with good will." The troops stiffen visibly nevertheless, and when Klaatu extends an object drawn from his uniform, one soldier fires, wounding him.

With a gasp, the crowd and military see Gort appear on the ramp, to the strains of his special musical signature. Bernard Hermann's inspired scoring for Gort's movements employed an unusual electronic musical instrument, the theremin, the sounds of which are made by moving the hands through the air in varying distances from two antennae. The dissonant, threatening waver of sound adds considerably to Gort's impact. He is the mechanical man, the servant, the companion, the accomplice. Gort took his place in screen history in the 50s along with Robby from FORBIDDEN PLANET — once the two best known robots in sci-fi film. They stand in a line of tradition reaching from the Golem, the METROPOLIS female robot, and Frankenstein's monster — the artificial man — to the computer Hal in 2001 and the STAR WARS robots.

The robot is the statue come to life, the Colossus of Rhodes. Gort's visor raises and an eerie bead of light sweeps across the slash of darkness. Then the ray fires: rifles glow and fall disappearing from soldiers' hands, a tank glows and is gone, a cannon. Gort was played by Lock Martin, who stood over seven feet tall, in an eight foot fiber-glass suit. A second, larger Gort head was built to perform mechanical operations involving the

The ray fires and a cannon is gone.

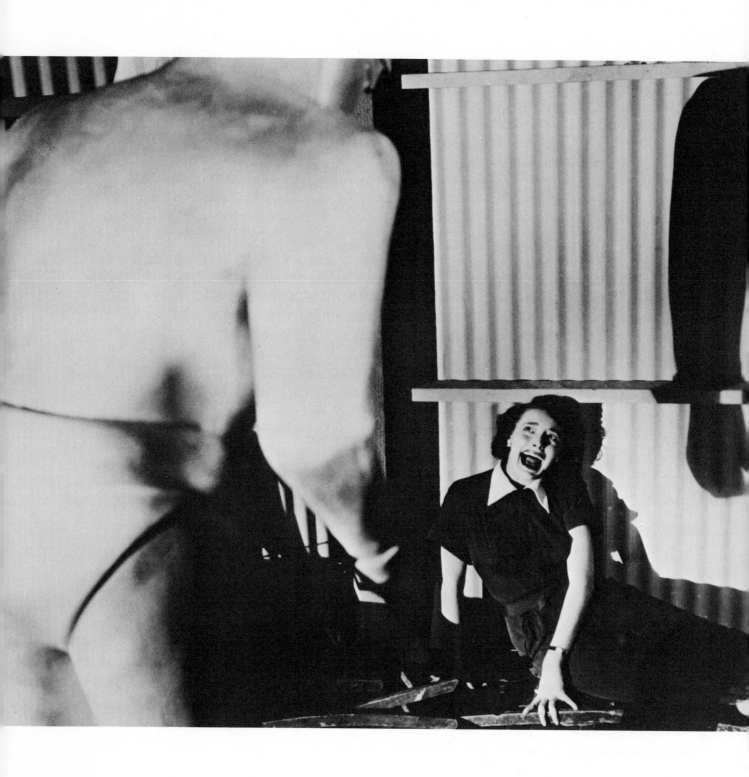

visor and lights. Scenes of the ray firing (using animation footage) took much of several months' time spent on optical printing at Fox studio labs.

Klaatu calls Gort off and stands, holding the object he has retrieved. He explains to the soldiers dryly, "It was a gift for your president. With this, he could have studied life on the other planets." At Walter Reed Hospital, the Secretary of Defense comes to see Klaatu. Klaatu says his mission is to address all the world's leaders on a matter of greatest urgency. The secretary explains such a meeting is impossible, considering the difficulties in international politics. In context, his hesitation is understandable. World tensions were at their worst point since World War II. The Korean War plunged the U.S. into armed conflict with the Communists, in 1950. The U.S. instituted crash civil defense programs. People bought and built bomb shelters and debated radiation shielding strengths. A story in the nation's newspapers quoted a minister saying a Christian might justifiably kill in defense of his bomb shelter. But to the international climate the secretary paints, Klaatu replies, "My mission here is not to solve your petty squabbles."

Klaatu decides he must spend some time with ordinary people in order to know the Earthlings and escapes from the hospital. Disguised in a suit of clothes belonging to a Major Carpenter, Klaatu makes his way to a boarding house, where he meets Helen Benson (Patricia Neal) and her son Bobby (Billy Grey). A tour of Washington with Bobby gives Rennie time to develop the gentility and bewilderment in Klaatu. Rennie, one of the few name actors to ever grace a sci-fi film, works up a genuine glaze in his spaceman's eyes as he stares out at Arlington Cemetery and remarks that where he comes from, "They don't have wars." His relationship with Bobby is one of three special encounters he has with the Earthlings. There is an almost immediate sympathy between Klaatu and the boy. At the Lincoln Monument, when Klaatu asks Bobby who the greatest man in the country is, he answers, "The spaceman."

The figure of the child is a classic player in science fiction, and Bobby helps Klaatu meet Barnhardt (Sam Jaffee), a classic sci-fi scientist. Klaatu has hopes Barnhardt can stir leaders of the world scientific community on behalf of his mission. In the 50s, the figure of the scientist was especially potent, held in esteem by the public, as well as viewed with apprehension. Klaatu tells Barnhardt, "We know you have developed a rudimentary kind of atomic energy. We also know you're experimenting with rockets. But soon one of your nations will apply atomic energy to spaceships. That will create a threat to the peace and security of the other planets. I came here to warn you that by threatening danger, your planet faces danger. Grave danger. I'm prepared, however, to offer a solution." Klaatu, unique in 50s sci-fi film, came to Earth to warn mankind against

As Gort's shadow falls over her, Helen cowers in terror.

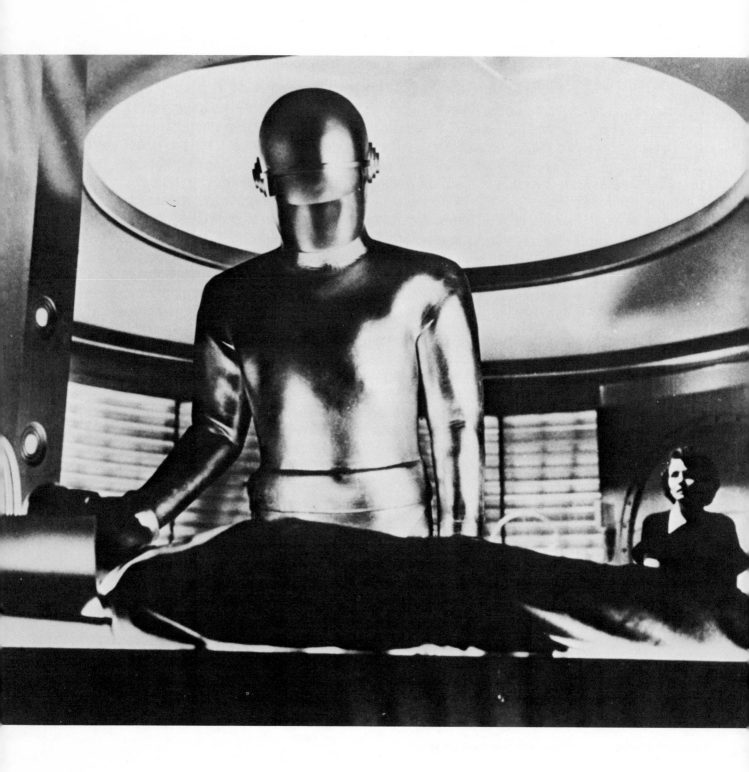

itself. Barnhardt tells Klaatu he must somehow demonstrate the force confronting humanity, and almost gleefully savors the prospects. Klaatu goes to the ship to make arrangements for his demonstration; Billy follows and sees him enter the saucer. What Klaatu arranges is the cessation of all power on the planet for thirty minutes, as though the Earth stood still. A montage of scenes carries us across the face of the planet as all human effort comes to a halt.

Klaatu and Helen inadvertently spend the thirty minutes alone together suspended between floors in an elevator, and she is persuaded to help. Helen's suitor also learns Klaatu's identity, and a chase through the city ensues. In a taxi, Klaatu tells Helen about Gort, "There's no limit to what he can do. He could destroy the Earth. If anything should happen to me, you must go to Gort. You must say these words: 'Klaatu borada nikto.'" When Klaatu is shot again, Helen flees to the saucer. Her face fills with terror as she sees Gort melt free from the plastic block and start towards her. Gort's shadow falls over her, her face fills the screen tremulously, and she is at last able to blurt the words out, the most famous alien talk of the decade. Gort carries her into the saucer, before retrieving the dead Klaatu from a jail cell. Inside the saucer, the 50s art-deco plastic control center is a splendor of lights and shadows, transparent cylinders and spheres. Klaatu's head glows in the rings of the resuscitation machine as though halos shine at his forehead.

Revived, Klaatu frees Helen at the entrance to the saucer and speaks to the scientists Barnhardt has assembled. His précis of the dilemma facing mankind makes for a ringing conclusion to the film. Before the saucer glows and rises to the night sky, Klaatu at last explains his mission: "I am leaving soon and you'll forgive me if I speak bluntly. The universe grows smaller every day and the threat of aggression by any group anywhere can no longer be tolerated. There must be security for all or no one is secure. Now this does not mean giving up any freedom, except the freedom to act irresponsibly. Your ancestors knew this when they made laws to govern themselves and hired policemen to enforce them. We, of the other planets, have long accepted this principle. We have an organization for the mutual protection of all planets and for the complete elimination of aggression. The test of any such higher authority is, of course, the police force that supports it.

"For our policemen we created a race of robots. Their function is to patrol the planets in spaceships like this one and preserve the peace. In matters of aggression we have given them absolute power over us. This power cannot be revoked. At the first signs of violence they act automatically against the aggressor. The penalty for provoking their action is too terrible to risk. The result is we live in peace without arms or armies, secure in the

Klaatu's head glows in the rings of the resuscitation machine.

knowledge that we are free from aggression and war, free to pursue more profitable enterprises. Now, we do not pretend to have achieved perfection, but we do have a system, and it works. I came here to give you these facts. It is no concern of ours how you run your own planet, but if you threaten to extend your violence, this Earth of yours will be reduced to a burned-out cinder. Your choice is simple: join us and live in peace, or pursue your present course and face obliteration. We shall be waiting for your answer. The decision rests with you."

Klaatu's fame has been enduring. Generations of movie-goers can now recite Patricia Neal's line to Gort. In the 70s, a rock music group named itself "Klaatu." Ringo Starr superimposed his face onto a studio publicity still and made Klaatu and Gort standing on the saucer rim into a cover for his record album, "Goodnight Vienna." In 1978, THE DAY THE EARTH STOOD STILL was the single science fiction offering from the 50s in the first major catalogue of feature films on cassettes for the new home video tape players. And nearly thirty years later, Klaatu's exhortation is still apt science fiction. Humanity is no closer to moderating the threat of its devastation, from its own awesome weaponry.

The saucer rises into the night sky and departs.

WHEN WORLDS COLLIDE

Chi/Con, Phil/Con, Cin/Con, Tor/Con, Lon/Con: science fiction conventions held in major cities across the country, and in other nations: Chicago, Philadelphia, Cincinnati, Toronto, London. Professional fans, writers, and editors commingling, often in costume. Learned discourse on the subtleties and nuances of the science fiction form. Heated debate, even argument, over the dénouement of a short story. Talk of the boom in science fiction publishing, dozens of magazines and scores of books. The mid or late 70s? Post STAR TREK and post STAR WARS? No, it was 1951. In the May 21 issue of LIFE magazine that year, writer Winthrop Sargeant went "Through the Interstellar Looking Glass" into the world of popular sci-fi, and scenes from new movies were included in his story: a full-page Gort carrying Patricia Neal through the shadowy corridors of Klaatu's saucer, Carrington's bed of hungry Things. And for the second time in little over a year, LIFE featured a new George Pal production. In April, 1950 the magazine had covered DESTINATION MOON; now it showed the space Ark from WHEN WORLDS COLLIDE.

Pal's success with DESTINATION MOON had helped set off the wave of sci-fi and space interest. And Pal's own prescience quickly brought his next project. Before DESTINATION MOON was completed, he had purchased an obscure property from Paramount studio and begun developing it. The property was a 1932 novel by Edgar Balmer and Philip Wylie, WHEN WORLDS COLLIDE, which Paramount purchased screen rights to in 1934 for Cecil B. DeMille. After DeMille picked CLEOPATRA instead, the novel languished for nearly two decades. When Paramount approached Pal about a sci-fi film, he was able to sell them back their own property and have two good laughs besides: Paramount was among the studios that originally turned down DESTINATION MOON.

Pal drew together a formidable production crew. From the earlier project, he brought Bonestell and composer Leith Stevens. His director, Rudolph Maté, had been cinematographer on the classic Carl Dreyer film, VAMPYR. Paramount's head of special effects, Gordon Jennings, already an Oscar winner for his work, was joined by Harry Barndollar. Al Nozaki and Hal Pereira, art directors, worked so successfully on the project that they, and Jennings, continued on with another Pal film at Paramount, WAR OF THE WORLDS.

The Balmer-Wylie novel provided genuinely epic material. While DESTINATION MOON

The huge space Ark under construction, looming over the base.

lifted people's eyes to the heavens, WHEN WORLDS COLLIDE brought outer space crashing down upon the Earth, in the absolute end-of-the-world. The story is standard disaster fare, but with a sci-fi twist, the destruction of the planet when another heavenly body crashes into it. The novel underwent the usual kind of Hollywood compression and restructuring. The head astronomer's daughter engages in some serious moral and philosophical talk with her two suitors in the novel; multiple marriages, polyandry, and genetics turn into a simple, if mild, 50s jilt in the movie. In a second novel, AFTER WORLDS COLLIDE, the authors relate the adventures of the colonists in the new world; the sequel was once a prospective project of Pal's.

The dimensions of the novel, and its Hollywood rendition, put WHEN WORLDS COLLIDE squarely in the grand end-of-the-world cinema tradition. The science fiction film has always been the ultimate disaster film, with its encompassing threat of unknown tomorrows. In 1910, Halley's Comet passed the Earth near enough to stir a film in which a comet destroys the planet. In 1933, DELUGE brought an earthquake and tidal wave that destroy Manhattan, in a fashion not unlike Pal's flood. WHEN WORLDS COLLIDE is commonly considered a standard setting depiction of the end of the world, but it did have its antecedents, as it had its descendents, Hollywood's disaster films of the mid 70s. The film's opening, in fact, harkens back to the very first "disaster" story of all. The Paramount mountain logo burns through to a solid sheet of flames, the credits run, and we see a leather-faced Bible turning open to a verse from Genesis, the first line of the story of Noah and the Ark.

A narrator speaks a line or two about astronomers and the search for answers to the mysteries of the universe, observatories far from the beaten path, and one more remote than any, "Mount Kena in South Africa." An astronomer — Dr. Bronson — has summoned a flyer, Dave Randall, to courier a mysterious case of photographic plates to New York City and a Dr. Hendron at Cosmos Observatory. The astronomers, science fiction's favorite scientists next to nuclear physicists, have discovered movements far distant from the Earth that will bring the end of the world. Before Randall even arrives in New York, he gets newspaper offers for the story of the box's contents.

When Hendron takes Bronson's findings to the United Nations, he is haughtily rebuked by another group of astronomers. Still, he insists: Bellus, a wandering star twelve times the size of the Earth, will crash into the planet completely destroying it in eight months; there is still time, though, to build a rocket, so that a few humans might escape to Zyra, a planet orbiting Bellus. The disbelief and debunking that follow in the newspapers and in Washington, D.C. are nicely summed up in a marvelous astronomer's line from the novel:

A tidal wave crashes through Times Square in New York City.

"Men aren't really educated up to the telescope, like they are to the microscope."

Dave Randall and the astronomers are thrown together and an infatuation develops. Richard Derr, another of sci-fi's unsung movie players, is Randall the flyer, a lady's man. As his plane approaches the observatory in the film's opening, it dives when he and a blonde inside kiss. On the airliner to New York, the stewardess eyes him. From their first meeting, he is after Hendron's daughter, Joyce (mercifully not "Eve," the new world daughter of the novel). In his best scene, Randall flirts with Joyce under the eyes of her other suitor, M.D. Tony Drake. Derr is a cross between Danny Kaye and Alec Guinness and a delight when he pulls a bill from his wallet and makes a small torch to light a cigarette; "money to burn" he calls it, with Bellus around the corner. Derr positively sparkles when he coos Randall's pet name for Joyce, "Stargazer." Barbara Rush as Joyce plays a standard sci-fi role. One of the few ways women got into the films at all was by being scientists; they also had to be tough, come what threats. Hendron's daughter assists his work and enlists the young women on the project, described as "all fine technicians."

Two industrialists who believe Hendron and Bronson get the project going with initial funds and a site at an old government proving ground. "Scientists Lease Mountaintop," reads a headline, as a crucial figure enters the drama, Sydney Stanton, an industrial tycoon confined to a wheelchair. John Hoyt gives a visceral performance as the self-serving, acerbic Stanton, a caricature who expects the worst, especially in people. It is Stanton who introduces firearms to the base, for what he says will be the inevitable struggle for the rocket; only forty some passengers of the several hundred persons on the project will make the flight. When his aide, Ferris, pulls a gun to insure his passage the last day, Stanton fires a revolver hidden in his wheelchair robe, killing him. For all the personal drama though, and competent acting, it is not the people we remember best in WHEN WORLDS COLLIDE. Pal wholeheartedly believed special effects could be the "stars" in movies. As in DESTINATION MOON, it is the marvel of space flight and the heavens that dominate the film, and the upheaval on Earth as the heavens draw nearer. The real excitement begins when Stanton says of the rocket, "Build it."

In one gripping shot we are transported from the human dimension to the interplanetary, when a bus enters the site and slides across the screen, revealing at a distance behind it the entire base: the rocket, the compound, the towering launch ramp. This startling scene immediately gives way to an even more powerful shot, the side of the huge space Ark under construction, looming over the base. Scenes of the rocket at the site combine live action footage of the construction area with a miniature rocket; in the side shots you can almost run a finger along an imaginary line joining the miniature

Bellus seen in the night sky above the towering ship's tail.

footage in the top half of the film frame with the live footage in the bottom half. A 700-foot length of the launch ramp was built full-size in Calabasas, California, in the San Fernando Valley west of Hollywood. Portions of the ship built full-size included an interior, 25 by 75 feet, an exterior side wall and entry hatch 100-feet long and 50-feet high, and a rear engine assembly. Scenes of the ship firing and launching, and the flight, used model animation and stop-motion photography, Pal's long suit again.

A red-framed, double-pad calendar begins the countdown: 79 days to passage of Zyra, 98 days to Bellus and the end. A lot of mileage is gotten out of ordinary footage of construction activity, livestock care, medical examinations, microfilming of books. (Balmer and Wylie used books between the walls of their ship as insulation.) While pages tear from the red calendar, workers pass under ubiquitous signs, "Waste Anything But Time." Now scientists around the world accept the group's early findings, though they remain skeptical about the ship. Foreign headlines scatter through scenes of evacuation and preparation throughout the world, as nations try to relocate coastal populations and brace for global dislocations. Across the country people are seen listening to the president's voice as he gravely intones there is no hope. Finally, one pad of dates has torn down to the last sheet, the word, "Zyra."

As the planet swings past the Earth and on into space, the world experiences a taste of what is to come. In the main bunker at the base, Hendron and the others wait nervously. Then it comes, a rumbling that shakes the room and begins a catalogue of calamities: fires, floods, torrential waves cresting over beaches, icebergs torn loose, volcanoes, streams of lava, exploding power plants, and most amazing of all, a tidal wave that crashes through Times Square in New York City. A good deal of these scenes were stock footage of natural disasters, but some sequences used miniatures: forests, railroad bridges, and cabins washed away.

The cataclysmic inundation of New York is possibly the most famous part of the film. Inspiration for the scene came from a remark by a studio publicist about what a wonderful ad could be devised from flooding Times Square. When Pal and the special effects crew produced the footage, the chilling image of the crashing wave became a keynote element in the movie's promotion. Blank plywood miniatures of the canyons of buildings at the intersection were built, approximately six feet tall; tanks of water were dumped into the landscape from different points and photographed. This footage was then combined with a single stock movie frame of Times Square that had guided construction of the miniature. Superimposition of the images provided the buildings' details, and hand-painted edges of the wave completed the effect. The startling aerial shot of the entire

The launch ramp lifts with grandeur up the mountain pointing skyward.

city — changed to sea in an exquisite nightmare — was a painting by studio artist, Jan Demila, but has been frequently attributed to Bonestell.

As the film neared completion, and word of its amazing scenes spread, Paramount played up the special effects for publicity purposes. The studio newspaper would note details of production activities in featurettes. For the sounds of earthquakes, sound men recorded large boulders rolling around in a tank of water, with a submerged microphone. For the Ark's launch, Paramount said arrangements were made for a sound crew (screened by the FBI!) to record — but not see — an experimental jet engine at Lockheed Aircraft Corporation. The trembling bunker room at the base was built on springs and then rocked up and down by pile drivers. Disaster at the rocket includes fires and the death of Bronson, when an overhead crane falls on him. (In the novel, Bronson is stabbed through the neck with a bayonet in an attack on the camp!)

The end is now literally in sight. A progression of Bonestell paintings shows Bellus growing daily larger; it fills the sky ominously, dwarfing even the towering ship's tail. Days slip away on the last half of the calendar. Randall and Drake make a helicopter foray with medical supplies for surrounding areas. In an astonishing moment they hang over the flooded New York City, and we see great ocean liners foundered among the tips of skyscrapers. They rescue a small boy who joins the camp. Randall jumps down to the rooftop of a flooded house and hoists the boy up. After a moment's hesitation Drake overcomes his jealousy and swings the helicopter back around for Randall, even though it means losing Joyce. In a further act of selflessness, Drake, as medical officer, is able to trump up an excuse for Randall's having to make the flight, to help pilot the ship.

After the last day lottery for places on the Ark, there is, indeed, an attack from the ranks of the base personnel. As Hendron and the others race to complete preparations and board the ship, workers find Stanton's boxes of rifles and storm the launch area; Stanton was right. In the last moments the sky is an eerie yellow from Bellus and windstorms whip up. At the gate to the rocket, workers open fire and scale the chain-link fence. With the last passengers on board, Hendron stands behind Stanton in his wheelchair. He kneels and throws the launch switch, dooming both Stanton and himself. He tells Stanton Zyra is for the young, and that they are the extra fuel they need. As the mighty engine roars to life and the Ark starts to slide away down the ramp, Stanton, horrified, jerks to his feet and stunned takes a few halting steps.

In the novel, there is an astonishing ferocity to the battle fought for the rocket. The mountain encampment between two of the Great Lakes is under siege by a marauding army of tens of thousands that streamed to the site at word of its existence. In the climactic

The space Ark's supreme moment, launch, blasting free.

struggle, the hordes overrun the base and the astronomers' party is forced to board the ship. Though the rocket is not yet ready for flight, its engines can be fired and it lifts offf vertically, hovering in the air, with its blast like a terrible blow torch. Balmer and Wylie write that the ship hung in the air thirty minutes, a horror of roaring flame incinerating the attacking thousands.

The Ark has been the supreme element in the film, all glinting steel blue and orange-red girders and trim. Now comes its supreme moment, launch. Bonestell's elegant rocket design carefully avoided the simple vertical take-off of the LUNA in DESTINATION MOON, as Pal wished, incorporating the unique, "mile long" launch ramp that lifts with grandeur up the mountain like a finger pointing skyward, heeding. As the very earth of the planet begins to fly up into the sky at Bellus' gravity, the Ark blasts free and into space. In the calming black of the heavens the small band sees the worlds collide on the ship's viewer. Randall brings the fuel-empty ship in through cloud banks and white crags to the "Best air I've ever tasted," he announces triumphantly in the hatchway. Zyra, like the letter Z, almost gone but not, a whole world gone but one beginning.

The concluding shot of the exotic new planet is notorious among sci-fi movie buffs who have attacked its saccharine cartoon quality. The scene is a Bonestell painting that was intended as a guide for the construction of a miniature Zyrian landscape. Paramount hurried the conclusion of the film, still in production when the Oscar for DESTINATION MOON was announced. A scene or two of action on the new planet was cut from the script, and the painting stood in for the model landscape. The hastily improvised ending was well enough received at preview screenings that the studio decided to leave the conclusion as it was. Pal and the production crew seemed to have outdone themselves, and packed off another Academy Award for special effects for WHEN WORLDS COLLIDE. And by the time of that Oscar, five crew members were already at work on a third Pal feature. Two times man had reached the heavens. For his third science fiction classic, Pal would bring company calling.

"Best air I ever tasted," Randall announces triumphantly.

IT CAME FROM OUTER SPACE 62

IT CAME FROM OUTER SPACE

"It's the desert. It gives people wonderful ideas." TARANTULA, Universal.

The camera passes over the empty landscape, combing the brush and horizon for some answer, some resolution to the receding blankness that is like the film's mystery. It begins to probe the face of the desert itself, and to question the sheer appearance of things. In the desert, as surely as nothing happens, anything can. The characters speculate: "It's alive. And waiting for you. Ready to kill you if you go too far. The sun will get you. The cold at night. A thousand ways the desert can kill." A telephone lineman: "After you've been working out on the desert fifteen years like I have, you hear a lot of things. See a lot of things, too. Sun in the sky. The heat. All that sand out there. Sometimes rivers and lakes that aren't real. And you think the wind gets in the wires and hums and listens." Against the stark desert backdrop, the action looms in heightened relief; the compelling clarity of events is liked the fabled clarity of desert sky said to draw the stargazer and his telescope.

In the late 40s and early 50s, the desert, the great American Southwest, stirred the fascination of the public. In Southern California, the aircraft industry grew dramatically with the impetus of World War II. East of Los Angeles, in the Mojave Desert, Muroc Air Force Base (later renamed Edwards AFB) was the site of research with new jet aircraft and where the sound barrier was broken by the experimental Bell X-1 rocket plane. In New Mexico, the "Land of Enchantment," scientists completed the first atomic bomb in the last days of the war at the secret U.S. laboratory at Los Alamos. In the southern reaches of the state, in the White Sands area around Alamagordo, the U.S. space program was begun with dozens of firings of captured V-2s. These remote stretches had a history of rocket launchings leading back two decades to the father of American rocketry, Robert Goddard, and his first experiments on the Mescalero Ranch east of Alamagordo in 1930.

In the context of the era's headlines, it is no surprise that a desert locale was a favored setting for sci-fi films. What better place for mystery, secrecy, and hidden doings, with featureless, unoccupied landscape for hundreds of miles in any direction, and hush-hush government installations tucked well out of public view. And what more likely place than the desert for flying saucer sightings? As humanity sought the heavens, might not alien intelligence seek out precisely the locations of space efforts? Might not extraterrestrials choose these same empty distances for landing strips and for similar

The eye of the astronomer, the fabled clarity of desert sky.

reasons, to come and go undetected? Since prehistoric time, the Southwest has borne the calling card of a momentous visitation from outer space, the Great Crater near Winslow, Arizona.

IT CAME FROM OUTER SPACE begins simply but auspiciously with two icons of 50s science fiction film, a practicing astronomer and an isolated small town situated in the desert. In a timely blend of elements and psychology, John Putnam of Sand Rock, Arizona raises his eyes skyward during a period when the U.S. as a whole was stricken with an anxious skyward gaze, from the specter of possible atomic attack, and the mystery of flying saucers. Harry Essex's bare-bones screenplay is credited as drawn from an original story by Ray Bradbury, "The Meteor." Universal studio approached Bradbury, who was then beginning to earn a name as a sci-fi writer, to come up with a subject for a 3-D sci-fi movie, but then assigned the actual screenplay to Essex. Bradbury's name was kept on the film, as was his idea of benign interplanetary visitors, but the story is Essex's.

IT CAME FROM OUTER SPACE was the first science fiction film done in 3-D, the briefly-lived 50s movie fad wherein movie-goers were treated to film action that jumped off the screen into the audience. The novelty film process was another of Hollywood's attempts to cope with TV, along with color, wide-screen, and increasing emphasis on spectacle in movies. In a special trailer for the film, lead actor Richard Carlson appears in a mist and explains that the film the audience is about to see is different from other movies. Objects will fly out of the screen and seem to hurtle into the audience. A brief animation sequence suggested what the sensation would be like, and showed how it was produced. Two movie images are actually shown on the screen, from separate projectors a distance apart, and the customary red and green plastic polaroid lenses synchronized the two images, producing the 3-D effect of depth in the image.

For a science fiction film, IT CAME FROM OUTER SPACE is commendably restrained, even noteworthy for its understatement. Considered as a 3-D film — that school of excess — it seems almost refined. Enthusiasts argue that it is the best 3-D movie. The stunning meteor sequence from the film's opening is enough of itself to reward repeated viewings, and would insure the film's lasting fame. The falling craft — a piece of dramatic action so essential in dozens of sci-fi movies — here receives an ultimate treatment in bulging 3-D. The sequence is so good, in fact, that it is repeated, almost three times. The film starts with the sequence run immediately before the credits.

The ship is first seen as a glowing meteor streaking across the top of the screen from the right; for a moment joshua trees rise and frame its path. As the craft streams closer to the Earth, skimming a distant ridge, it begins to rush headlong into the camera. In one of

The ship is first seen as a glowing meteor.

the most masterful moments of 3-D in the movie, and in all 3-D film, the fiery ball fills the screen, as we make out for the first time the strange hexagonal-patterned grid on its surface. Only after the meteor has crashed to Earth and smoke and debris billow up from the crater do the title and credits run. Moments later, after a brief interlude with Putnam and his friend, Ellen Fields (Barbara Rush), in his backyard on a spring night, the craft falls again, with even more exaggerated 3-D effect. At the film's conclusion, the ship leaving the planet is actually the beginning of the sequence used a third time, printed with the negative reversed, so that the meteor is seen streaking away from the Earth, left to right across the screen.

The ease with which the fireworks, the hardware, are gotten over early in the film tells us we are in sure hands. The mastery of IT CAME FROM OUTER SPACE lies in its less-is-more strategy. A quiet, confident film, it makes small commotion about things. The meteor is simply the beginning, however tempting the 3-D impulse. Similarly, the extraterrestrial "Xenomorph" — literally, "foreign form" — is brought on immediately, dispensing with suspense. Before Putnam arrives at the crater with Ellen, the ship eerily hums and quietens and the camera passes into its darkened recesses to confront the grotesque, protuberant eye creature in gorged 3-D. Then we see as the space Cyclops sees, out a kind of fishbowl lens that rings and distorts the screen. The disagreeable aliens are given a musical signature in Herman Stein's score that presages their movements, a shrill, struck-violin keening that is used several times to effectively substitute for their actual appearance. It is an accomplished film, indeed, that puts its cards on the table in just a few first minutes.

The authority of the film is such that it brooks even self-mockery, moments when the action pokes fun at itself or deflates tension. In a striking 3-D effect immediately following the meteor fall, Putnam swings the great eye of the astronomer, the telescope, from right to left and wildly out from the screen, in a humorous, even witty parody of the craft's course. When Putnam sees two aliens walking in town disguised as missing telephone linemen, they give themselves away by holding hands. At the telescope, Putnam exclaims the meteor has fallen near an old mine (the Excelsior — "Ever Upward") and sets off with Ellen for a helicopter ride to the torn and steaming crater.

The towering latticed orb is perhaps the most powerful image in the film. The crater scene of the glowing ship dwarfing Putnam's figure silhouetted in the smoke and dust is one of the most famous film visions of human and alien contact. The enormity of the globe and the awesome mystery it holds combine in a spectacular single moment. The evocativeness of the image is so great we never forget its brilliance and majesty,

The great latticed orb in the crater.

though we see it only once. Scenes of the ship employed a miniature whole globe and a full-scale section of the globe wall and craft entrance constructed and built into a rock wall at the desert location, some fifteen miles north of Hollywood. The exalted figure of the ship was a curious anticipation of the familiar Buckminster Fuller geodesic domes two decades later. The obligatory 3-D rockslide occurs sensibly when the aliens cover over their craft. At the crater's rim, Putnam tells Sheriff Matt Warren (Charles Drake) what he saw, "Some kind of ship, like nothing we've ever seen before, a huge ball rammed there in the side of the crater." He also claims he saw something inside the craft, before the unsettled wall caved in.

In classic 50s flying saucer story terms, Putnam undergoes an instant but thoroughgoing cultural debunking. Like dominos, the sheriff, reporters the next day at the 1000-foot diameter crater, Professor Snell — an astronomer from nearby Wayne Observatory — the Army, one by one all discredit his story. He is discredited on the radio — "publicity seeking astronomer" — and in headlines — "Stargazer Sees Martians." Putnam, who insists on his knowledge, navigates two conspiracies: the mystery of the alien ship, and an ever-widening circle of disbelief. He wildly exclaims to Ellen: "They've talked about me before. Snell agrees with the sheriff, the sheriff agrees with the others, I'm crazy." In a word, Putnam's vision and predicament become paranoid: the world is allied against him because of what he has seen. When the aliens begin to "borrow" a number of humans and chameleon-like assume their form to move about unobserved, Putnam's plight becomes even more desperate.

The first abduction takes place at the recurrent setting in the film, on a stretch of desert highway. Two phone linemen are engulfed by a gaseous mist in the cab of their truck. George, the dissembling younger lineman (Russell Johnson), gives himself away to Putnam when he stares blankly at the sun and remarks peculiarly about its being beautiful. When Putnam hurries away, the real lineman wakes to see himself, as the xenomorph explains: "Don't be afraid. It is within our power to transform ourselves to look like you." Putnam faces both xenomorph-linemen in a darkened hallway down an alley in the town and is told the aliens mean no harm but must have time or terrible things will occur. More abductions follow: three prospectors near the mine, Snell and his assistant. Ellen is abducted when Frank, the older lineman (Joe Sawyer), appears in front of her car on the highway. Her scream as he enters the auto turns into the jarring ring of a telephone in the sheriff's office.

Putnam is lured to the crater, where an Ellen-xenomorph in a shoulderless cocktail dress appears on a hillside and draws him to the mine entrance to speak. She explains their

Down a darkened hallway two aliens in human form.

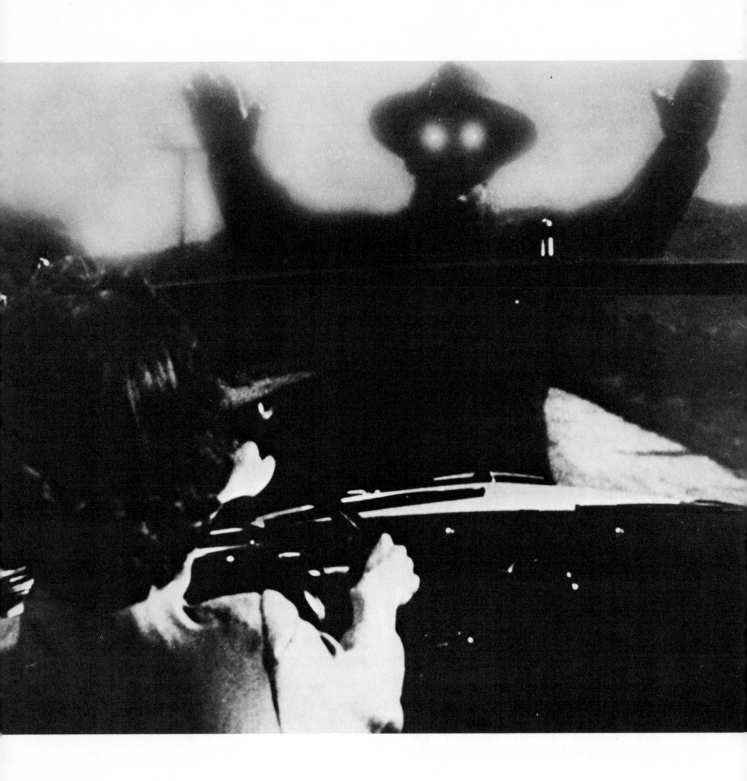

presence on Earth is an error and that they are repairing their ship in order to resume their journey to another world. The xenomorph says they have adopted human form to avoid frightening Earthlings with their appearance. Prompted by Putnam's insistence, the xenomorph reveals its true form. Putnam is nearly undone by the visage but resolves to help the aliens, and keep the townspeople away from the area until nightfall, when the ship will be ready to leave. At his house, he finds evidence of a xenomorph visit: clothes missing from a closet, and leading away into the desert brush, the wafting, glistening trail the aliens leave, like enormous silver snails. Mounting antagonism between Putnam and the sheriff climaxes in a fight in the sheriff's office, as Putnam prevents him from stopping and questioning one of the linemen who was reported missing. He races to the mine in the sheriff's car ahead of the townspeople marshaling at barricades on the highway.

Putnam enters the mine and is met by the Ellen-xenomorph again. One of the aliens has been killed on the highway and she says, "You can't be trusted anymore," opening fire with a lethal ray that scores the rock wall behind Putnam as he ducks. The 3-D beam streaming out of the screen is made up of fireballs that are miniatures of the xenomorph craft, complete with tiny hexagonal patterns. Putnam fires a handgun and a second alien is killed, falling into a chasm. The close call with the sinisterly alluring Ellen-xenormorph in the mineshaft is very much like the experience Miles Bennell has in INVASION OF THE BODY SNATCHERS three years later, when a Becky-pod impersonation turns on him in a cave.

Putnam hears machinery and makes his way to a central chamber where he finds the ship, the hostages, and the party of xenomorph-humans. Work on the craft is underway; a beam cannon mounted outside fires into the ship in an exotic repair operation. Leading the aliens is a second Putnam, standing at the device. Like a textbook diagram of a classic paranoid and his fears, Putnam confronts himself as the two speak. In a last gamble, the xenomorphs are persuaded to release the hostages. They flee the mine and Putnam sets off dynamite, sealing the entrance from the sheriff and men gathered outside. The Earthlings hear an ominous rumbling inside the mine and see debris begin to fly up from the crater. The ship blasts back up into the sky, departing peacefully at last. The film ends optimistically on Putnam's wistful note, "It wasn't the right time for us to meet just now. There'll be other nights, other stars for us to watch. They'll be back."

Producer William Alland and Director Jack Arnold's success with IT CAME FROM OUTER SPACE began a series of sci-fi films for the two. Together they made such other 50s favorites as the CREATURE FROM THE BLACK LAGOON movies. In TARANTULA, Arnold returned to his favored desert setting with a monstrously over-grown

Ellen is abducted in the night on the desert highway.

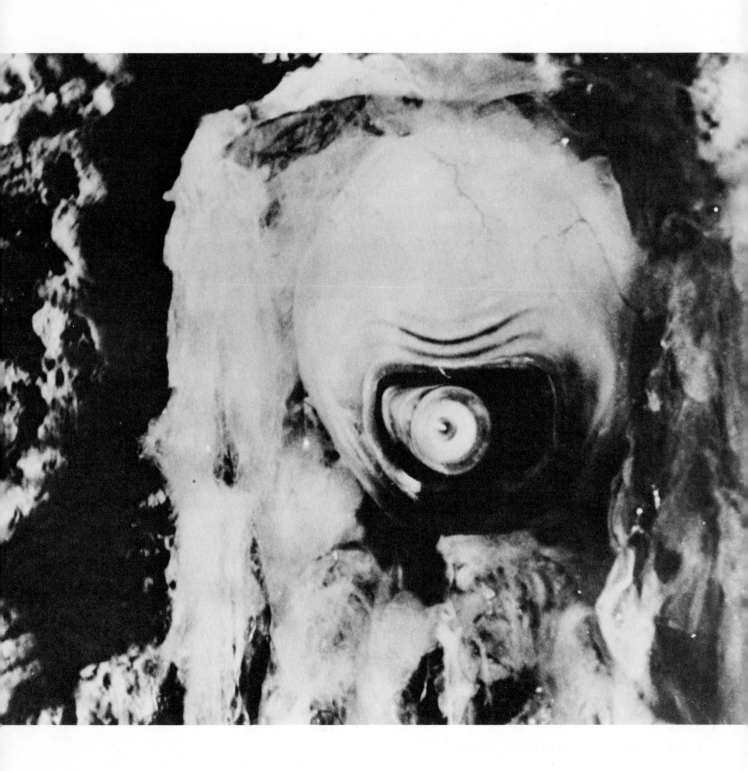

spider. THE INCREDIBLE SHRINKING MAN, Arnold's other contribution to the school of dislocation-of-size sci-fi, was a genuine departure for the genre, with its disappearing hero. MONOLITH MONSTERS, another desert tale of ruination from a meteor, was from a Jack Arnold story, and used the falling meteor sequence from IT CAME FROM OUTER SPACE, cut just before the appearance of the hexagonal pattern. Arnold is also said to have directed uncredited scenes in Alland's THIS ISLAND EARTH.

It is conventional wisdom now that the 50s' bumper crop of sci-fi movies was a stand-in anxiety for the decade's paranoia, but few of the movies were as articulate as IT CAME FROM OUTER SPACE in its exploration of the threat of veiled conspiracies. No matter that Putnam was right, and not mad. The film offered a distorted and fit mirror of the times, when Sen. Joseph McCarthy tallied numbers of communists in the government in newspaper headlines, and people speculated that even flying saucers were disguised atomic panic. Fear, threat, and conspiracy were abroad in the land, even unto TV. In 1953, the year IT CAME FROM OUTER SPACE was released, Richard Carlson also starred in the TV series, I LED THREE LIVES, the documentary story of Herbert A. Philbrick's communist impersonations as an FBI counterspy.

The Xenomorph, the extraterrestrial eye creature.

INVADERS FROM MARS

William Cameron Menzies, the director of INVADERS FROM MARS, is a landmark figure in the history of science fiction movies, as well as in film generally, an artist and illustrator who greatly influenced design in the new American film industry. Menzies' essential contribution was his practice of turning a written screenplay into a body of illustrations that rendered the entire appearance of a film, as well as guided its production. In a career spanning nearly forty years, Menzies won the first award for art direction from the newly formed Academy of Motion Pictures in 1928 and designed GONE WITH THE WIND in 3000 color sketches. His special feeling was for films of the fantastic and romantic. In 1934 and 1935, Menzies designed and directed THINGS TO COME, from the H. G. Wells novel, the second certifiable masterpiece in sci-fi film. The magnitude of the film's vision overwhelmed audiences with its cities, vistas, and imposing space gun. The enormous production staff included 200 special effects crew-members alone.

In the context of his career, Menzies' work of 1953, INVADERS FROM MARS, seems a miniature but its special place in sci-fi film is secure, nonetheless. INVADERS FROM MARS has become a cult movie, one of those strange, underground obsessions that stir a dedicated following; it is a recurring favorite at sci-fi conventions and stirs lengthy discussion in fan circles. Professional fan magazines run twenty and thirty page retrospectives on the film, including dozens of photographs. The fact that a prestigious film figure like Menzies directed an independent, minor effort like INVADERS FROM MARS is but a part of the unusual history of the film.

Producer Edward Alperson's plans for a film about an invasion from Mars were prompted in part by the general sci-fi movie boom, and in part by publicity surrounding another Mars invasion film in production, George Pal's WAR OF THE WORLDS. INVADERS FROM MARS beat WAR OF THE WORLDS out by six months and did good box office business, but not without considerable misadventure. The producer hired screenwriter Richard Blake to revise the original story by John Tucker Battle, essentially condensing it. What had been a planet-wide attack became an isolated attack on a small town where an atomic rocket is being built. When the ending of the story was changed, Battle disassociated himself from the project and insisted his name be taken off the movie.

With production about to begin, Menzies lost his comprehensive "storyboards," two

David sees a glowing in the trees at the hill.

months' artwork that illustrated the entire movie. When final footage was several minutes short of the minimum length necessary for distribution, sequences in the existing film were repeated. The Martian mutants seem to lope back and forth in their tunnels in a peculiarly monotonous fashion because the same footage was used over and over, printed with the negative reversed. The endless montage of scenes repeating the entire movie at the film's climax was another concoction to add minutes to the movie. More minutes were later added to the film for European distribution.

INVADERS FROM MARS is the definitive sci-fi movie of the child, a picture that centers on the point-of-view of a young boy. From Bobby in DAY THE EARTH STOOD STILL to the little girl in THEM, the figure of the child is an important and recurring element in sci-fi film. The child is a potent figure of identification, always a version of ourselves. In the perspective of science fiction, the magic, invention, and excitement of a child's world is like the promise of unpredictable tomorrows. The child can believe anything, and tomorrow is where anything can happen. Tomorrow makes children of us all. Man becomes smaller in the face of the unknown. We are only seed in the universe, we might only be atoms. The child's fragile place in the world is like humanity's fragile place in time and in the universe. The stars are our fathers; they do not come from us.

INVADERS FROM MARS is the story of David MacLean and his adventures when a flying saucer lands behind his home. At the film's beginning, we are thrust immediately into the precariousness of a child's world. We see a small town and a single house, a sandhill rising behind it. David (twelve-year-old actor Jimmy Hunt), an amateur astronomer, wakes at four in the morning to view the constellation Orion from his bedroom window. After his parents settle him he stirs a second time and sees a glowing in the trees at the hill; it is a flying saucer. It moves from behind the trees into view before disappearing beneath the sandhill; a crust of earth covers over the glowing green dome. David rushes to tell his parents who assure him he was dreaming. A special predicament of the child is getting adults to believe him. Until well into the movie, David undergoes remonstrations at his story; worse, there is something wrong with the grownups around David.

Battle's original screenplay incorporated an important idea in science fiction, the control of human behavior by aliens. The Martians overpower humans in the movie and control them through surgical implants in the backs of their necks. David's parents, policemen, a little girl and a succession of humans fall victim to the Martians, all while David is unable to do anything about the spreading plot. It is another version of the assumption of human form by aliens, like the chameleon improvisations John Putnam saw in IT CAME FROM OUTER SPACE, but even more sinister. Now humans perform the wishes of the aliens

A flying saucer disappears beneath the sandhill.

and move one step closer to the ultimate horror, becoming aliens themselves. David's terror is like Putnam's terror, at the very surface of things that can no longer be trusted to be what they seem. Battle's idea came in part from a childhood nightmare remembered by his wife, who dreamed her mother was not really her mother. The special threat of human impersonation occurs again and again in sci-fi movies, but nowhere more frighteningly than in the case of the child who must suspect his parents. It is the first paranoia.

With David back in bed, we overhear his parents. His father works as a design engineer on the rocket at Coral Bluffs Proving Ground; there have been rumors at the base and he'll take a look outside. The sandhill behind the house is the dominant image in the film. We return to it again and again, as the humans disappear into its mystery. It is where the Martians are hidden and where the story reaches its climax. As George MacLean heads up the path, we hear the "theme song" of the hill, an acapella chant of a dissonant, eerie four-note melody by a choir of sixteen voices.

Each time the hill is about to claim another victim, we hear the evocative, otherworldly voices. MacLean reaches the peak of the hill and stands at the fence as the voices crescendo. In the soft blue of pre-dawn the sand of the hill begins to slide and cave in, funneling, forming a deepening whirlpool. Then MacLean drops abruptly out of sight and the sand closes. The whirlpool effect, designed by Menzies, was accomplished by applying a vacuum hose to a slit in the stretched canvas that supported the sand of the hill set. In the morning, David's mother calls the police when MacLean hasn't returned, and two patrolmen are similarly abducted.

Suddenly the father returns. His glazed, perspiring face fills the screen as he stands in his robe and one slipper, blankly explaining he stopped off to see someone. David stands behind his father and sees an unusual x-shaped cut in his neck. He asks about the cut and his father turns snarling, knocking him down; he is not himself. The two policemen reappear and David sees the x-scar on their necks. They ambiguously agree with MacLean that the episode can be forgotten. Shortly after, MacLean takes David's mother to the hill. Behind the house David sees a little girl drop into the hill.

David tries to phone his friend, Dr. Stuart Kelston, at the observatory, and then goes to the police station. He enters running down a stark, unrelieved hall towards the desk sergeant. David charges up to the figure of authority seated between the upraised light globes, in a foreshadowing of his standing beneath the Martian Intelligence and beating on the pedestal of the transparent sphere. David speaks with the police chief, and terrified, sees the x-scar on his neck; the chief claps him into a jail cell to be held for his parents.

David runs down a stark, unrelieved hall towards the desk sergeant.

The sergeant, bemused at the behavior of the chief, phones a Dr. Pat Blake to see the boy. In an unintentionally funny moment, David asks to see the back of her neck before telling his story. The MacLeans show up at the station but in the meantime Dr. Blake has reached Kelston, and refuses to let David go with them. MacLean warns David about his story and barks, "He's been reading those trashy science fiction magazines. He's completely out of control."

Pat takes David to the observatory, where Kelston tries to phone General Mayberry, commander at Coral Bluffs. Shots in this sequence show Palomar Observatory, northeast of San Diego, California. Palomar, with its newly installed, giant 200-inch telescope — the world's largest — caused great excitement in the early 50s; it must have been irresistible to include stock footage of one of Southern California's newest wonders, the enormous Hale telescope rising as the entire dome turns in slow grandeur. The image is like a hand-tinted 40s postcard of Southern California. Kelston asks David what planet is closest to Earth at the time; David answers Mars and the three talk theories of Martian life. Kelston describes an underground Martian civilization and mutant slaves that is remarkably like the scene inside the hill. They focus the telescope on the rocket at Coral Bluffs and then turn it to the hill, where they see MacLean lead General Mayberry to his abduction.

Kelston phones the Pentagon and talks to a Colonel Fielding, introducing one of sci-fi film's most durable and omnipresent actors, Morris Ankrum. Ankrum was the epitome of the sturdy military leader, at his best, as here, ordering up the firepower. Arthur Franz, as Kelston, is another of the era's recurring players, but Ankrum's arguably the best known face in sci-fi movies. INVADERS FROM MARS is extreme in its display of military hardware, even considering the tenor of the 50s: packed horizons of parked tanks, trainloads of tanks rolling across countrysides, tanks clanking along and tanks taking position. Interspersed with live action are fully five distinct sequences of Army stock footage, until the appearance of the armored vehicles becomes actually funny. (A strident "Caissons Go Rolling Along" in the soundtrack accompanying the tanks doesn't add to their sobriety.)

Fielding and his aide Rinaldi meet with Kelston, David, and Pat at the MacLean house. Rinaldi climbs the path on his own and is pulled down into the sandhill. The others watch through binoculars as he fires his rifle down into the hill and disappears. Fielding growls, "We may have no counterweapon, but if it's a fight they want, they're going to get it." Night at the hill finds soldiers and armor massed to join battle with the Martians. The

Colonel Fielding leads the first soldiers into the Martian tunnels.

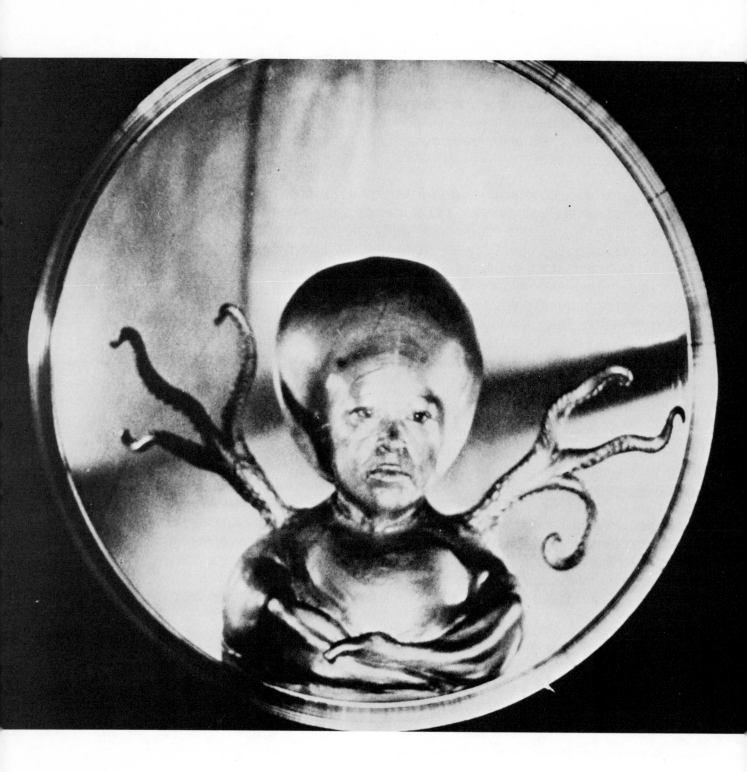

abducted little girl dies mysteriously of a cerebral hemorrhage and the military obtains one of the crystal neck implants to use to trace the signal.

The implanted police and General Mayberry are killed in sabotage attempts against the rocket. David's parents are captured near a lab after a shooting and taken to a hospital where surgeons will attempt to remove the implants. Abruptly, David and Pat are pulled down into the hill. The military blast an opening into the hillside where they disappeared, and Fielding and the first soldiers enter the confusion of the Martian tunnels, standing in the strange green light of the bubbled walls. (Menzies' design for the odd spheres bunching on the tunnel walls was implemented using ordinary rubber prophylactics!)

David and Pat lie at the feet of the towering Martian mutants, who then carry them through the tunnels to the inner chamber. A transfixed Rinaldi says of the horror in the transparent sphere, "He is mankind developed to its ultimate intelligence. These are his slaves, existing only to do his will, as you will." The appearance of the Martian Intelligence carries out Battle's original conception of the creature as an overgrown brain entity with vestigial body features, the winking tentacles. Menzies' hand comes to the fore in the Martian interiors: the elegant, stylized central chamber with its sparse air of refinement, the shimmering transparency of so much of the set. Menzies' ideas articulate rather than fill space; the few Martian accoutrements seem to give way to the air. There is an odd feeling of tentativeness to the design, which heightens the tension. The "empty" economy of the sets worked handily in the cost-conscious production. Menzies emphasized depth in his approach to the film which was once planned for 3-D.

The mutants were played by one Max Palmer, a circus giant who stood eight feet six inches, and Lock Martin, Gort in DAY THE EARTH STOOD STILL. Because so much of the activity of the roles was physically difficult for the large men, four normal-sized stand-in actors performed most of the mutant action scenes in the struggle, with stand-in midget actors playing soldiers. Luce Potter, a woman midget, played the Martian Intelligence, standing on a box in her streetclothes, face made-up and fitted into the sphere structure. As the eyes of the Intelligence dart silent commands, the mutants force Pat to a table and the implant device begins its implacable descent from the heights of the chamber.

The needle tip draws nearer and nearer the back of her neck. Kelston and the soldiers shoot their way in, rescuing Pat and David, and set a time bomb. David has seen the mutants operate a ray weapon; he and a soldier fire it, melting the walls of a tunnel and making good the escape. The bomb face looms larger and larger as David runs down the slope of the hill, and sees the whole adventure flash before his eyes.

The eyes of the Intelligence dart silent commands.

Here begin two different versions of the film's conclusion. In the original film David thrashes in bed as the explosion occurs, ending the montage of scenes. It was all a dream and he goes back to sleep, until he wakes to see the saucer again, and the film ends. Six months after its U.S. release, the ending was changed and more footage shot for European distribution. The saucer explodes taking off and Kelston and Pat put David to bed, sans dream. The reasoning was a dream ending would not play well with European audiences. For even more realism, several additional minutes of talk at the observatory were shot, expanding the scientific discussion about Mars and including a display of kinds of flying saucers. The definitive version of the film, edited in 1976 by a film distributor making new prints, combines the additional observatory footage with the restored dream ending.

It is fitting that the "dream" nature of the movie remains enhanced at the ending. Like a dream and like the world of a child, INVADERS FROM MARS has an unreal quality: overly rich colors, the uncanny choir of voices, the automaton daze of the controlled humans, even the ghostly pastels of the Army tanks footage. It is a fairy tale grown up, a 50s spell with an enchanted, primitive authority. As David gazes out the window one last time the whole drama is set in motion again, unendingly ringing in the mind. It is always the end of autumn on the hill, the spirit of a year has passed through. In the fall school begins, you feel very young, the trees teach a lean lesson about paths in life. The atmosphere of the hill is heavy, pungent; leaves are burning somewhere, even though there are Martians.

The implant device begins its implacable descent from the heights of the chamber.

WAR OF THE WORLDS

The surface of Mars at last, home of the trouble-makers of the Solar System, the neighborhood sore spot, red with exacerbation from countless tales of its threatening denizens. The real mystery of Mars is why does it have its special fascination? Thousands of years before Christ, people knew Mars rose in the sky. It was one of the five planets recognized by the first astronomers in Babylonia and Egypt. The Greeks and Romans named the planet after their god of war, because of its red appearance; in the Nineteenth Century its two moons were discovered and named after the horses that pulled Mars' chariot, Deimos and Phobos — terror and fear. Because there is little atmosphere on Mars, we are able to see its dramatic, changing surface: an orange and red rust color with dark "canal" markings and white polar caps. The very first movie aliens were Martians, in A MESSAGE FROM MARS, a stage play filmed as a movie in 1899, and there have been more movie aliens from Mars than anywhere else. The most famous Mars story is, of course, WAR OF THE WORLDS, by science fiction great H.G. Wells.

WAR OF THE WORLDS has been incarnated countless times, in forms ranging from comic books to paperbacks to pop music record albums, and on three especially memorable occasions. In 1897 in England, readers first thrilled to Wells' novel serialized in PEARSON'S magazine. Forty-one years later, the evening of October 30, 1938, Orson Welles and his Mercury Theater broadcast a contemporary radio script of the story that convinced thousands of Americans that Martians had actually landed in New Jersey. The Halloween radio show was scandalously successful, prompting public outcry at its overly authentic nature. Fifteen more years later, in 1953, the most sensational WAR OF THE WORLDS appeared, a new George Pal science fiction thriller.

Two years in the making, at twice the cost of DESTINATION MOON, WAR OF THE WORLDS was certain to be remarkable from its beginnings. Paramount had owned the movie rights to the property for 26 years before assigning it to the estimable Pal. He drew immediately from the production crew of WHEN WORLDS COLLIDE, art directors Nozaki and Pereira, composer Stevens, special effects man Jennings, and artist Bonestell. Byron Haskin, the director, had once been head of special effects at Warner Bros., bringing even more technical wizardry to the assembled talents. Haskin and Pal formed a relationship that extended through three more sci-fi films.

The surface of Mars at last.

From the outset, emphasis was on special effects, and even new heights of movie magic. Fully half of the film involves some form of special effects. Live action shooting took forty days and cost $600,000; special effects cost nearly the balance of the film's budget, and took nearly a year's work. Pal even wanted 3-D. The death rays and haunting Martian craft were made for the 50s film novelty, but Paramount ruled otherwise. Pal even suggested a compromise, the last reel of the film; scientists at the A-bomb drop putting on their smoked glasses would cue the audience to put on their 3-D glasses. Almost predictably, WAR OF THE WORLDS became the third George Pal sci-fi film to win an Oscar for special effects. By the end of the decade, Pal was the acknowledged dean of sci-fi movie makers.

Partly due to the rash of flying saucer sightings in the country, Englishman Barré Lyndon's screenplay moved the story forward in time from England in the 1890s to contemporary Southern California. Bonestell's work begins the film, a remarkable two and a half minute tour of the Solar System that begins with Mars. As the camera pans slowly across the canals and a distant Martian city, actor Sir Cedric Hardwicke provides a Wellsian voiceover that explains the planet is dying and the Martians must migrate. A succession of Bonestell paintings shows the planets the Martians have rejected, and then a meteor is seen falling through the sky and crashing to Earth, outside Linda Rosa, California, a small town about thirty miles east of Los Angeles.

In the commotion of townspeople at the steaming meteor, Dr. Clayton Forrester (Gene Barry) drives up, an astro-nuclear physicist camping nearby with two other scientists from Pacific Technical Institute. He meets Sylvia Van Buren (Ann Robinson) and her uncle, Pastor Matthew Collins (Lewis Martin). Forrester is curious about strange characteristics of the meteor, including its radioactivity, and decides to stay until it has cooled. While the townspeople and Forrester enjoy a square dance that evening, three stragglers at the meteor first encounter the Martians. After the stately prologue the pace quickens and never slows down. The entire action of the film takes place in a little more than 24 hours, ending the dawn of the second day. The first meteor appears on a Saturday night and by nightfall Sunday the Earth is doomed.

The opening of the meteor is an episode from the novel included in both the radio and film versions; the drama of the unscrewing threads is unmistakable, with their sinister grating sound. (For the turning screw threads, Orson Welles' staff improvised an agreeably ominous scraping sound with a pickle jar submerged in a toilet bowl.) When the lid falls free, a sinister metal head rises up into view. The metal stalk's ticking and steamy hissing give way to the most threatening sound of all, the throbbing beat of the blistering ray as

"I shall dwell in the house of the Lord forever."

it disintegrates the three men. The ray streams headlong into the camera engulfing them, turning the screen a burning white. The ray fires again when Forrester and police reach the scene, disintegrating a fleeing auto.

What we are being treated to are image combinations from different film exposures, made on an optical printer, a mechanical process that essentially superimposes one image onto another in a single frame of film. Film can also be run and exposed with portions of frames masked and left blank, rewound and rerun later to expose the masked areas, providing combinations of imagery. Individual frames in the film included as many as 24 different exposures. In these first scenes of the ray firing what we are actually seeing is footage of live action and of melting welding wire shooting from the blast of a blow torch. The first stalk seen was a full-size, ten-foot metal apparatus from Al Nozaki's design. The pulsing light in the face was produced by a fan blade turning in front of a light bulb in the stalk head. Sounds of the ray firing were recordings of electric guitars played backwards.

Forrester and a policeman hide in a ditch and see a second meteor fall. They summon the military from El Toro Marine Base, under the command of General Mann (Les Tremayne), who greets the scientist with an obligatory atomic reference, "Clayton Forrester. I haven't seen you since Oak Ridge" (Oak Ridge, Tennessee, site of a key facility in the development of the atom bomb). We hear meteors have fallen through the night in Santiago, London, Naples, and that the Linda Rosa meteor was apparently the pilot ship. Because the military has been able to dig in here, the Linda Rosa site will provide a good test of the strength of the Martians. Forrester speaks to a newsman about the Martians, and in a familiar montage we see the faces of the public scattered across the country hearing the broadcast. (If we look carefully, we even see the same group of plain folks gathered near an iron coal stove that listened to the president in WHEN WORLDS COLLIDE!) At dawn, Sunday, the forces will join battle.

Sylvia and Pastor Collins are at the encampment with Forrester, and by dawn, the Pastor is disturbed about the military preparations. At first light one awesome Martian ship appears rising out of a ravine, and Collins steps out to meet it, in another of the episodes drawn closely from the novel. The pastor walks towards two ships now with his Bible raised in his hand. The cowboy steps into the street and faces the sun glinting on the other's holster. The Bible inside his leather vest will stop the bullet. For a moment everything is still, like before every death. Collins is reciting the 23rd Psalm, "I shall dwell in the house of the Lord forever." The beaded pulse of the Martian craft sounds again and the minister is disintegrated. The Bible stops nothing. Gods from another planet.

The experimental Northrop Flying Wing used as the atom bomber.

The ensuing tour-de-force Martian attack is a rout for the humans. As the military opens fire, protective "blisters" appear over the craft, transparent bell-jar shapes. Nothing touches the ships. We see a litany of military hardware disintegrated in dazzling reds and yellows, part of nearly 4000 painted film frames combined with live footage. The crafts' wingtips begin to fire another kind of devastating ray. A military leader charges into the bunker and we see an incredible sequence of his body disintegrating, the screen filled with his skeletal structure glowing in the candescent green and blue. This brief piece of film magic took some 140 individual painted figures.

In the midst of the fireworks, the gleaming, sculpted ships are stately, even tranquil in their slow, airy glide. Nozaki's design for the crafts came in a sudden, inspired solution to the problem he and several of the production crew were working on. Originally, concepts from the novel were pursued; the craft was a gigantic tripod as Wells described it, an enormous, walking milking stool. What Nozaki struck on was a manta ray shape, free of legs, that moved on force beams. In an early experiment during production, "ray" legs were tried out and photographed successfully, but the electrical set-up was too dangerous to be used. When the very first ship appears at dawn, the few shots of the blinking ray legs can be seen.

The crafts were three models 42 inches across and 22 inches high. Wood frames were wrapped in appropriately reddish copper foiling and filled with a maze of wiring that controlled movements and lights. More than a dozen control wires suspended and powered the ships which hung from overhead tracks. The bottom half of the craft that crashes at the end of the film was the only full-size mock-up. The crafts were a pride to the entire production crew, down to the hundred or so that sprinkled world maps in military chart room scenes; these tiny miniatures quickly disappeared from the set as crew members' mementoes. (Like other excellent props in movies, the ships turned up later in another film, ROBINSON CRUSOE ON MARS, directed by Haskin.)

Forrester and Sylvia escape the debacle in a small Army observation plane. They make their way to a farmhouse which is then struck by another meteor. The two pick their way in the demolished structure and see a craft descend in the yard outside. Another kind of mechanical arm extends from beneath the ship, a three-lensed viewing head. When it finds them, Forrester chops it off with an axe. The darkness seethes with the sounds of the craft looming outside as shadows creep behind Sylvia and Forrester. A grotesque three-fingered hand reaches and touches Sylvia's shoulder.

As she screams, Forrester turns his flashlight on it, the sole Martian in the film, a furtive, spindly

One of the war craft advances on Los Angeles City Hall.

creature, smaller than a human with a sickly, red-pink oversized head. It cringes and throws its arms up to its face, covering a bulging three-lensed eye, each lens a color like the viewing head, red, blue, green. Air tubes designed over its body provided an unpleasant pulsing appearance. The Martian is only a small part of the movie, though the farmhouse episode is one of its tensest scenes. What the Martian did provide was the threatening image of the hand, which became part of advertising artwork, the three sucker-tipped fingers grasping down out of the air.

The voice of Cedric Hardwicke intones again as fiery dots fall towards the Earth: "It was the beginning of the rout of civilization, the massacre of humanity." Montage footage carries us across the face of the planet as the superimposed Martian crafts wreak their relentless havoc. In Washington, D.C. it is clear there is no alternative but to use man's ultimate weapon, the atom bomb. A decision is made to drop it on a concentration of Martian ships at Linda Rosa, before the crafts advance on Los Angeles. Forrester and Sylvia reach Pacific Technical Institute, where the scientists are able to spend a few precious moments examining the optics of the viewing head and the Martians' peculiarly anemic blood, found on a cloth in the farmhouse after Forrester struck the creature with a two-by-four. They leave shortly for an observation post near the target.

A particularly unusual feature of the film was the experimental Northrop Flying Wing used as the atom-bomber. Air Force stock footage was used, interspersed with the tense preparations of the military and scientists. Rare scenes of the Wing taking off and in flight add special drama and grandeur to the film. Northrop built approximately twelve of the enormous planes, prototypes with a variety of bombing and reconnaissance capabilities. At one point, they might well have been adopted by the Air Force, substituting for what became the familiar U.S. bomber fleet of B52s. But the skies over Viet Nam were not to fill with the Flying Wing, and all existing planes were destroyed.

As the Wing banks overhead, the bomb falls to no avail. Through the turbulence and mounting storm of the blast — a 75-foot high explosion devised on a studio sound stage — the intact Martian ships are seen advancing. Civil defense forces evacuate Los Angeles as the Martians approach. Forrester and the scientists race to pack equipment for further study of the Martians' blood. A bus of the scientists sets out in the chaos as the attack comes, and Forrester is separated from them.

After his truck is taken by a rampaging mob of looters, he wanders through the streets searching for the scientists. The final moments of Los Angeles' destruction are a horrendous splendor: lines of the ships proceeding down the streets, the unceasing volley of the rays. A craft advances on Los Angeles City Hall and fires, as an eight-foot

Los Angeles City Hall and the unceasing volley of the rays.

City Hall miniature explodes. The devastation is complete as Forrester runs seeking Sylvia. He finds her in a church as a stained glass window explodes shattering over their heads. Outside the church another explosion fills the air and then silence, as one of the ships is seen crashing into the side of a building. Dumbstruck, Forrester approaches the hatch that has opened down out of the ship's bottom. The hand again, withering, the three sucker fingers gripping and pulling the arm toward the hatch edge.

Another ship falls and Forrester says, "We were praying for a miracle." Bells begin to peal. Hardwicke explains the Martians were killed by bacteria, germs that man had long been immune to. We see fallen ships before the crumpled Eiffel Tower, in Rio de Janeiro, at the Taj Mahal, as he speaks: "The end came swiftly. After all that man could do had failed, the Martians were destroyed and humanity was saved by the littlest things which God in his wisdom had put upon the Earth." The film ends with Los Angeles in dawn light, Monday morning, light from the horizon even as flames and smoke rise across the distance. The last scene is framed by a church spire rising on the left, and filled with the chorus of a choir. It is one of science fiction's great lessons, and was Klaatu's lesson: humility. Though man might smash the atom, and reach for the stars, before the unknown tomorrows he must ever stand humble.

A fallen ship before the Taj Mahal.

BEAST FROM 20,000 FATHOMS

"Who's ever seen a dinosaur? You can get away with murder, making a dinosaur walk." RH.

H. G. Wells, Fritz Lang, William Cameron Menzies — and the great movies associated with their names — all exercised influence on some of the finest sci-fi films of the early 50s. It is not surprising that many of the films were great achievements, if we consider the antecedent figures in their development. In the history of fantastic cinema, and science fiction film, there is no figure that casts a bigger shadow than KING KONG and his creator, Willis O'Brien. The history of model animation in movies more or less begins with O'Brien, as does the history of BEAST FROM 20,000 FATHOMS. O'Brien was experimenting with short subjects using animated miniature models and stop-motion photography as early as 1914. In 1925 he completed THE LOST WORLD, a Sir Arthur Conan Doyle story of prehistoric life, the first feature film using model animation. In 1933 his masterpiece, KING KONG, took the world by storm, the first sound feature using model animation. Even today the film is hailed as the finest hour of model animation. It would be two decades before anyone, or any films, appeared worthy of being called the successors of KONG and O'Brien. It would be, in fact, an O'Brien protegé, Ray Harryhausen, who carried on the high tradition of miniature magic.

Ray Harryhausen's first fascination with the art of model animation came to him as a young boy, making clay models from the painted murals of prehistoric life at the La Brea Tar Pits in Los Angeles, near his home. When he saw KING KONG, it was the turning point in his life, no matter his tender age of thirteen. He devoted himself from that occasion on to a mastery of the discipline, to bringing to life the dinosaurs in the paintings that so captivated him. His first efforts at animation and stop-motion photography as a teenager were so primitive they were attempted with a camera with no stop-motion device! Time brought practice though, and a deft hand. By the early 40s he had a reel of film starring a stegosaurus that was good enough to get him work as an animator with George Pal, then establishing his animation studio and beginning his PUPPETOONS series. And Harryhausen was at last in direct contact with O'Brien, who also worked a while at the Pal studio. In 1946 O'Brien hired Harryhausen to be his assistant on another giant ape movie, MIGHTY JOE YOUNG. After two years of animation work, almost all of it Harryhausen's, the film was released and won the 1949 Oscar for special effects.

Harryhausen was ready now for bigger things, his own first feature film. In 1952, he was

A second man sees the beast loom up and bear towards them.

BEAST FROM 20,000 FATHOMS *100*

meeting with producers and screenwriters on a film project called "Monster from Beneath the Sea." Plans for the monster had evolved to some form of prehistoric life when by happy circumstance a Ray Bradbury story appeared in the SATURDAY EVENING POST, "Beast from 20,000 Fathoms." Bradbury, then a rising sci-fi writer, was an old and close friend of Harryhausen's. They'd grown up together as teenagers in Los Angeles and belonged to the now famous Los Angeles Science Fantasy League in the 30s and 40s. Harryhausen was best man at Bradbury's wedding. Bradbury wrote the introduction to Harryhausen's book of memoirs, FILM FANTASY SCRAPBOOK, recalling with delight the animator's garage full of boxes of monsters. The producers bought the story and the title, even though it consisted of one short episode: a forlorn, wandering sea serpent hears a lighthouse foghorn and comes lowing to it in reply; in its agitated loneliness it demolishes the lighthouse. The scene became part of the completed screenplay, which included Harryhausen's idea for a grand finale, the monster at Coney Island amusement park in New York City.

BEAST FROM 20,000 FATHOMS, the first 50s dinosaur movie, set off a sub-genre in the sci-fi movies, the rampaging monster not from outer space but of an Earthly, usually atomic, origin. The precise nature of the monstrosities varied greatly from film to film, but the dinosaur was always a favorite figure. Eugene Lourie, director of BEAST, did two more dinosaur movies himself, THE GIANT BEHEMOTH (with Willis O'Brien) and GORGO. Harryhausen turned out more saurian epics, including a combination of cowboys, dinosaurs, and wonderful lassoing sequences, VALLEY OF GWANGI. Two years after BEAST FROM 20,000 FATHOMS its most infamous imitator was set loose on the world, GODZILLA, KING OF THE MONSTERS, from Toho Films in Japan. GODZILLA was the greatest international success of Japan's film industry and set off that country's plague of radioactive, sci-fi movie monsters. The dinosaur holds some special fascination for people, perhaps because it is the reptile. From the Loch Ness monster to the serpent in Eden, the dragon — the walking snake — is a figure of archetypal potency. Fairy tales and children's books abound with dinosaurs.

Harryhausen's "Rhedosaurus" was an original, a combination of characteristics from a number of prehistoric saurians; no real dinosaur was thought to look fierce enough. Designed and constructed by Harryhausen, the model was just under a foot tall and three feet long. It was built up of rubber and plastics over a steel ball-and-socket-joint frame that articulated a miniature skeleton in authentic detail. The finished model was both pliable enough to be moved into different positions, and rigid enough to hold different positions. Two models of the rhedosaur's head in a larger size were made, essentially

The beast rises up beside the lighthouse in silhouette and tears it down.

hand-puppets, to provide greater detail in full-screen close-ups of the beast seen through the windows of a ship's cabin and lighthouse tower.

The film was a remarkable one-man tour-de-force. Harryhausen worked entirely alone, as he has on most of his films, because of the concentration required for the painstaking positioning and repositioning of the model, in steps of fractions of inches. He did his own lighting, ran his own camera, and performed all the animation of the rhedosaur. For nearly seven months the stop-motion photography proceeded, frame by frame. Using a variety of optical procedures the miniature footage was then combined with live action footage. In his first 50s films, one of Harryhausen's most effective approaches involved projecting live action footage in miniature and photographing it with the model.

Harryhausen's most consistent technique has been his use of models in one way or the other. He frowns on live lizards, say, as dinosaurs, or actors dressed in costumes as monsters, or giant, mechanically-operated monsters. For more than forty years he has perfected an art of miniatures finer than clockwork; they are lifelike. (Harryhausen once told a NEW YORK TIMES reporter that his film, TWENTY MILLION MILES TO EARTH, included 500,000 positions of its creature, the Ymir.) In 1963, ten years after the sea monster piece, another Ray Bradbury story in SATURDAY EVENING POST celebrated one Terwilliger, a magician of a movie animator clearly modeled after the author's friend, Harryhausen, and the poetry of his "Thunder Lizard."

BEAST FROM 20,000 FATHOMS begins in a familiar setting, the snowbound reaches of the arctic north. A ship lies anchored in a plain of ice as a voiceover details the last moments of countdown to H-hour in "Operation Experiment," an exercise in nuclear detonation. We overhear two personnel: "Every time we let one off I feel like I'm writing the first chapter of the new Genesis." "Let's hope we're not writing the last chapter of the old!" A plane hangs in the sky, an enormous blast fills the screen, as well as the 50s' familiar mushroom-shaped cloud. Scientist Tom Nesbitt (Paul Christian) speaks briefly with Colonel Evans (Kenneth Tobey) before setting off in a small half-track for the blast site.

The men are dots in the white; the landscape obliterates everything. They come to a standing instrument and take some readings. Then one man sees a moving form and fires a signal shot. A dark shape passes between two rises of ice, with a row of fins rising along its back like teeth. There is a dull, ominous roar. A second man sees the beast loom up and bear towards them. "A monster. A prehistoric monster," gasps one to the other, before falling ice crushes them. Nesbitt, the lone survivor, claims he saw the monster and winds up in a hospital in New York City. As a "psychiatric interrogation" into his "traumatic

The beast steps in toward the central city crushing automobiles.

hallucinations" begins, Evans comes in and tells Nesbitt he discreetly left the monster out of his report. But Nesbitt remarks, "No wind ever sounded like that."

Off Newfoundland, Canada, in the Grand Banks area of the North Atlantic, a small tug makes its way. It is night, vision is obscured. Three men in the small cabin peer into the gloom. Suddenly the head of the beast appears through the window, so close it fills the screen. The ship is lost in the violent thrashings of the beast and Nesbitt reads about it in the hospital, an article about a crackpot sea serpent sighting. He goes to see a Professor Thurgood Elson at an ivy-covered university. Cecil Kellaway gives a marvelous performance as the plump, absent-minded professor, given to shaking his head quizzically over things.

Elson is a world-regarded authority on prehistoric life and even he disputes Nesbitt's claims. He says such a creature would be over a hundred million years old and could not possibly still exist. Nesbitt speculates it was trapped frozen and the bomb melted the ice freeing it, an unexpected side effect of the nuclear doings in the north. The atom affects the past as well as the future! Leigh Hunter, the professor's assistant (Paula Raymond), listens to all of this; she used to be Elson's student. When Nesbitt goes, she comments about Nesbitt's brilliance and how he was received in this country for his acclaimed research on properties of radioactive isotopes; this explains Nesbitt's — and Swiss actor Christian's — European accent. During this scene, a person in the background mounts a scaffold before an enormous dinosaur skeleton. The person stands suspended at the top of the giant rise of the backbones. The confusion of the scaffolding framework and bones suggests a roller coaster ride at an amusement park.

Another ship is reported lost amid sea serpent reports and Leigh goes to see Nesbitt at his office at the Atomic Energy Commission. That night the two of them pore over pictures of dinosaurs. Finally, Nesbitt spots the rhedosaur. The two go to a small Canadian village seeking the captain of the second lost ship, but he has fled the reporters and the curious. A second survivor in a nearby hospital identifies the rhedosaur too, and they return with him to Elson's lab. Elson now talks out of the other side of his mouth. He is interested. He says a deep-water drag of the Hudson Subterranean Caverns 150 miles north of New York brought up bones of the rhedosaur; the area could be its nesting grounds, prehistorically old.

Elson phones Colonel Evans about his concern, but the officer puts off even the world's foremost paleontologist. It takes one more episode before Evans will move to help the scientists. It's the Bradbury story scene, the beast and the lighthouse, set off the coast of Maine. Two men inside the towering brick candle pass the time, one with a concertina;

The beast towers in the narrow confines of Manhattan's streets.

it is just like inside all the lighthouses in the world. Then the beast rises up beside the lighthouse in silhouette and tears it down, eloquent, brute testimony to the marvel of Harryhausen's fingers.

Elson stands before maps and charts with Nesbitt, Leigh, and the military. He traces the beast's course south along the Arctic Current. He points to the beast's destination and says they must go down into the canyons of the Hudson Caverns to find it. At sea, preparations are completed to lower a bell into the water. Elson begins the search of the hundred mile long trench as the bathysphere hangs in the depths ever so much like bait on a fishing line. When the professor spots the rhedosaur he cannot believe his eyes. He is elated and begins describing him, "He's enormous . . . definitely a paleolithic survival," until we see the beast swing its head near the bell and begin to open its mouth. At the surface, Elson's voice is abruptly silent. The beast has taken the bait.

Harryhausen managed this sequence without a drop of water hitting his model, filming a miniature sea canyon through a water glass — two panes of glass joined with water between them. This well known "fishing" sequence got special treatment in some of the first release prints of the film. To highlight the eerie drama of Elson's descent into the deeps, footage was tinted green; tinting was an occasional film novelty before the eventual refinement of color processes.

A newspaper heralds, "Famed Scientist Lost in Sea Tragedy, Mystery Surrounds Cause of Disaster." Then the beast comes ashore in New York. It appears dockside and sets off a terror in the shipping yards. Crowds scream and flee as it steps in toward the central city, crushing automobiles and lashing its tail into buildings. It towers in the narrow confines of Manhattan's streets, smashing against the walls. Its head peers in through a suite of windows high in a skyscraper, aping KING KONG. It reaches down and snaps up a policeman in its mouth, tossing him down as it rears back up. It picks up a car in its mouth and shakes it like a toy, while a horrified man bangs around inside. Havoc reigns a fraction of an inch at a time, at the masterful hands of Harryhausen.

Troops pour into the streets. Nesbitt and the military at a rooftop command post watch the beast attack a barricade at nightfall. A bazooka shot wounds it in the neck and great drops of blood spot the streets. Soldiers begin to stumble and fall, one by one victim of some virulent plague, a hundred million year old germ now free too. Nesbitt says they cannot destroy the beast with shellfire, infection would spread. Its ashes would be infectious, too, if it were burned. The only thing to do is shoot a radioactive isotope into the wound and kill it with radiation poisoning that will destroy all the diseased tissue.

Nesbitt and a sniper must go up onto the roller coaster to get a clear shot.

The climactic scene, Harryhausen's grand inspiration, takes place at the roller coaster ride in Coney Island amusement park. One roller coaster miniature was built entire, standing five feet high, for the fire that ends the movie; for shots of the beast thrashing about in the structure, smaller sections of the coaster were devised. Harryhausen usually has considerable influence on the screenplays for his films, as he is the first and last word on just what can be done with animation. His ordinary approach is to sketch a number of key scenes that a script is tailored around. In this instance, Nesbitt and a sniper must go up onto the coaster to get a clear shot at the beast's wound, two ghostly figures in radiation shielding suits riding up the coaster in a car.

The white planking and structure of the coaster are skeletal in the floodlights, the dips and rises look like a graveyard of monstrous creatures. There is death everywhere. The two men stand at the top of the structure as the beast rages across from them. The coaster car rolls forward away from them and rattles jarringly on its way as the sniper tries to aim; then it crashes where the beast has torn up tracks and the structure begins to rise in flames. For an instant we see the pulsing blood in the beast's wound. The sniper fires the isotope from a rifle grenade launcher and the two men make their way down the coaster. The beast and the coaster structure both go quickly, collapsing together as though kindred.

Warner Bros. had big plans for BEAST FROM 20,000 FATHOMS. It was a sci-fi natural and its way had even been cleared a year earlier by a successful re-release of KING KONG. The film was "premiered" simultaneously in 500 cities beginning June 1, 1953, and within three weeks had nearly 1500 bookings throughout the country. Warner Bros. was practically mass distributing the film, rather than area by area as customary. VARIETY reported the studio was spending as much on promotion — $200,000 — as it cost to make the movie, with heavy emphasis on TV and radio advertising. It was, in fact, one of the first instances of planned saturation marketing. And it worked. It was the surprise money grosser of the year. Harryhausen tinkered further with the rhedosaur in some experiments with model animation in 3-D, but soon turned to other creatures. With the lesson of the beast full upon Hollywood there were soon droves of outlandish monsters careening over the landscape. BEAST FROM 20,000 FATHOMS was but the first cry of Nature in revolt. Reeling from the various invasions from outer space, humanity now faced the very planet it inhabited rising up in calamity. Science had pushed the Earth too far with the atom. It began pushing back.

The white planking of the coaster is skeletal in the floodlights.

THEM

"Even an ant is the beginning of a new universe." Children's proverb.

For Hollywood and the modern science fiction film, the future began rather precisely with the end of World War II. Two startling developments during the accelerated technological efforts of the war pointed dramatically forward. Rocket research on the German V-2 put humanity on the threshold of space and the explosion of the Atomic Bomb began the nuclear age. Outer space, or the inner workings of the atom, one or the other dramatic element dominated most 50s sci-fi films. And for all the saucer sightings, certainly the atom represented the nearer of the two futures. The entire world had witnessed the bombings of Hiroshima and Nagasaki, and blinked. The beginning of the 50s rang with the atom, as though it were a tolling bell. In a curious turn of history and geography, research on both the atom bomb and rocket flight took place in the same isolated stretch of a hundred miles in Southern New Mexico. West of the location of Goddard's rocket launchings on the Mescalero Ranch and the area that became White Sands Missile Range, in the wastes of the Jornada del Muerto desert, U.S. scientists exploded the first atomic bomb in 1945.

The secret research team went to the Jornada because there was no one there. Spanish conquistadors searching for the fabled Seven Golden Cities of Cibola named the desolate reaches in the Sixteenth Century. The "Journey of Death" lies halfway between Albuquerque and the Mexican border, east of the Rio Grande River. Sixty miles further east is Alamagordo, known as "Rocket City" in the 40s. The test area, known as the Trinity Site, became part of White Sands Missile Range. On the morning of July 16, 1945, the desert of the "Journey of Death" lit up with the scientists' efforts. One scientist said the gigantic blast looked like an enormous churning brain. Two parties of the researchers rolled into the blast area in lead-lined tanks. Awe-struck, they reported at the center of the explosion a crater 100 feet across and 25 feet deep, filled with melted grains of sand, ceramic, emerald green glass, the famed "Pearls of Trinity." It looked like a swollen jade blossom in the desert surface; it was the flowering of the new age. Some time later in Oscuro, New Mexico, at the "Atomic Bar," tourists could dip their hands into a quart jar of the beads, "Trinitite."

In these same locales nine years later, THEM begins, with joshua trees, the desert elders, the wise men of the tribes of sand. They frame the screen through the credits and then a

The six-year-old actress gets the best and most famous scene.

111

plane flies between them. A police car and the plane are investigating a peculiar report when the pilot spots a small child walking in the brush. A little girl is stepping along blankly carrying a doll with a piece missing from its forehead. The two officers in the car take the entranced little girl with them to a reported disturbance at a trailer and automobile nearby. The side of the trailer has been torn violently open. Officer Ben Petersen finds the missing piece of the doll's forehead in a cabinet, but no people. With a lab crew working over the wreckage, the officers prepare the girl in an ambulance. A shrill clicking sound fills the air for a moment, and the girl sits up stiffly on the stretcher. The ambulance driver says, "It must have been the wind. It's pretty freakish in these parts."

The two policemen stop at Gramp Johnson's general store at dusk as wind comes up. The store is shattered. They step tensely through the wreckage as a radio somewhere in the store blares jarringly. A shotgun is found with the barrel bent into a right angle. In the beam of a flashlight Gramps is found at the bottom of stairs into the cellar, lying with his face and chest torn and bloodied, in piles of glistening white sugar crawling with ants. Petersen notices the walls of the store are pulled out, not pushed in, like the sides of the trailer, and leaves his partner, Blackburn, to keep watch. The clicking noise begins again, drawing Blackburn through the store and out past a window. We hear shots and his screams.

At the police station, Petersen (James Whitmore) greets Robert Graham (James Arness), an FBI agent from Alamagordo. The little girl's father, missing from the trailer, was an FBI agent vacationing with his family. The county medical offier reports a peculiarity in the autopsy on Gramps Johnson; his body was full of enough formic acid to kill twenty men. Graham sends a plaster cast of strange tracks found at the trailer and store to Washington, D.C. A telegram in reply alerts the men to the arrival of two scientists, entomologists Howard and Pat Medford.

At the airport, Petersen and Graham are nonplussed when Dr. Pat Medford climbs down a ladder beneath the airplane and catches her skirt, showing some leg. She is Patricia, the daughter Medford (Joan Weldon). Edmund Gwenn as Dr. Howard Medford is textbook perfect as the patriarch scientist, customarily rounded with the comfortable weight of age. At the police station he asks questions before a map of the area; we see the name "White Sands" prominently. Medford asks where the first A-bomb was set off. He's told in the same general area, White Sands. He says, "Nine years. It's genetically certainly possible."

Medford then asks to see the little girl. The six-year-old actress gets the movie's best and most famous scene. Hers is that performance distinguished by compression, how

"It's gigantic. Over twelve centimeters. Over eight feet. This is monstrous."

much is done with how little. She has been mute so far in the film, in her three scenes. Now she is to have her single word of dialogue, the unforgettable cry of "THEM!" — the film's title. The scientist leans down and holds a vial in front of the child's face. She sniffs and blinks, bursts from her chair and cowers in a corner, shrieking, "Them! Them! Them!" Sandy Descher, as the little girl, is one of the best known children in all of sci-fi film.

The special mystery of the title was a key-note of the film's promotion: "A horror-horde so terrifying there was no word to describe THEM!" To the public it was: "T-error, H-orror, E-xcitement, M-ystery." To the theater industry it was: "T-he H-ottest E-xploitation M-ovie of the year!" Expanding on the successful promotion of BEAST FROM 20,000 FATHOMS the year before, Warner Bros. claimed record advertising saturation and provided some of the first extended movie film clips for TV promotion. Studio pressbooks included dot-to-dot coloring contests and "Them Fighter" armbands for children. In the spirit of the times, theater managers were urged to contact Civil Defense agencies and arrange tie-in exhibitions in theater lobbies: "What would you do if (name of city) were attacked by THEM? Prepare for any danger by enlisting in Civil Defense today!" Similarly, the military could be contacted for possible assistance: "Show 'Em Bazooka! Local armory might be willing to lend you a sub-machine gun, bazooka, flamethrower, and grenade rifle — weapons used in the film. Strap them to lobby board or behind roped off area and explain that these weapons were no match for THEM."
The studio made a publicity bother, too, about secrecy precautions surrounding the production — the precise nature of THEM — including when the film crew worked on location in the Mojave Desert, thirty miles from the nearest town, in the Palmdale area north of Los Angeles.

With the little girl's reaction, Medford is seized anew with urgency and asks to be taken to where the trailer was found. Wind beats up as the party dons sand goggles and surveys the terrain. Medford suddenly points and drops to his knees — the tracks: "It's gigantic. Over twelve centimeters. Over eight feet. This is monstrous." In short order we see what the doctor envisions. A gigantic ant appears over a rise directly above Pat, waving its head back and forth, clacking its mandibles hungrily, and making the clicking noise. Medford directs them to shoot for the antennae and Petersen manages to kill the ant with a machine gun. Medford makes clear his worst suspicions: ". . . a fantastic mutation probably caused by lingering radiation from the first A-bomb." He explains the formic acid in an ant's stinger, hideously oversized at the bottom of the mutant ant, that was found in the dead victim. And it was formic acid that he wafted under the little girl's nose in the hospital. He says they must find the nest immediately, or they may be too late:

A helicopter search of the desert locates the nest.

THEM 116

". . . witnesses to a Biblical prophecy come true. And there shall be destruction and darkness come across creation and the beasts shall reign over the Earth."

As far as the movie going public was concerned, Medford couldn't have been righter. THEM was but the "A" of an entire alphabet of atom-gorged species the sci-fi movies would spawn. THEM set the standard for the insect genre, and was also a classic of the dislocation-of-size sci-fi movie. Inevitable pretender offspring included (all oversized): TARANTULA, THE DEADLY MANTIS, THE BLACK SCORPION, THE SPIDER, MOTHRA, MONSTER FROM GREEN HELL (30-foot queen wasp), and MONSTER THAT CHALLENGED THE WORLD (caterpillar). In THE FLY, perhaps the most disagreeable insect movie of all, a scientist accidentally swaps heads with a fly in a molecule transporter.

It was all insect fear, seized on with inspiration by the radiation-enlightened movie makers. Who doesn't understand insect fear? All those things under rocks, in cobwebby boxes in garage corners. Dig down in flower boxes and see what happens. And those sun-crisp mornings you walk into a kitchen and see the sink drain a perfect lace of ant thousands, in through the window or a seam, tracing back and forth in the extended webs of traffic lines. Combs and hives of insects, bits of brain tucked into porch rafters. George Worthing Yates' first sci-fi story foray met with such response that he worked on eight more sci-fi projects, including CONQUEST OF SPACE for George Pal and two with Ray Harryhausen.

A helicopter search of the desert locates the peculiar hillock of the nest. Two ants stir at the opening of the hole. One holds a human rib cage in its mandibles and drops it down the rise of the mound. The bones roll down to join others, and a deputy's gunbelt and revolver, the missing persons. The ants, full-size mock-ups, were surprisingly effective for the little activity they actually engage in. Prop master Dick Smith supervised the construction of the mechanical ant rigs. There were two "lead" ants, one complete giant, and one minus its hindquarters mounted on a dolly for mobility. A crew of more than a dozen prop men ran the ants with a system of wires, pulleys, and levers. There were also ant "extras," heads and pairs of antennae that would wave back and forth when blown by wind machines.

The ants were a purplish green, for the production was originally set for color photography. Two days before production began color was cut from the film's budget. The film's original producer, Ted Sherdeman, was also dismissed from the project shortly before filming began, but remained credited for screenplay. Both circumstances were

"This is it. The queen's chamber. The eggs."

THEM 118

examples of studio skepticism about the movie — which became Warner Bros.' biggest money grosser in 1954.

Wisely the ants are kept in darkened surroundings, almost entirely underground, in shadowy tunnels. Here they work with an unpleasant menace that makes up for authenticity or liveliness. Though "effects" in the film were limited to the ants and encounters with them, these sequences were regarded highly enough to earn the picture an Academy Award nomination for special effects. THEM and the Harryhausen films nicely juxtapose film making alternatives in bringing monsters to life, full-size and miniaturized. The nest is shelled with poison gas during the heat of the day when the ants are thought to be all inside. Then Petersen and Graham escort Pat down into the nest for evidence Medford says they must have to confirm the ants have been destroyed.

The unnerving descent into the nest brings another close brush with an ant, fought off in the narrow tunnels with a flamethrower. Deeper and deeper the three go, following the ant passageways at Pat's direction. The gas piles and eddies at their feet like fog; it provides an atmosphere of moors, London nights, old horror mixed with the new. Finally they enter a room and Pat says, "This is it. The queen's chamber. The eggs." She photographs the dull white larvae which we see next in pictures that Medford holds. The worst has happened: "They've gone on their wedding flight." Two queens and their attendants were not in the nest with the rest of the colony. When Medford is asked about their flying range, he says ordinary ants have been found in the stratosphere.

In Washington, D. C. Medford briefs a group of military leaders about the facts of ant life. He shows a movie about ants and a glass ant farm display. He says ordinary ants have an industry and ferocity that make humans look feeble by comparison. Ants are the only creatures in the world beside humans who make war. If the two queens are not found and destroyed, man as the dominant species of the planet will be extinct within a year. The military goes on a national observation alert. We see a tender-aged Leonard Nimoy — a later generation's TV Spock — carrying a telegram to a desk. Graham and Pat go to see a flyer in a hospital who reported seeing "flying saucers that looked like ants." Crotty, the flyer, is Fess Parker, TV's Davy Crockett in the 50s. One nest is located aboard a ship at sea; we see an ant attack a sailor at a radio. The crew of the ship is lost and a cruiser sinks the hapless freighter.

A large sugar theft in a train yard brings the search to Los Angeles. Following arrest leads in the area, Graham and Petersen interview a drunk drying out in a hospital. He happily tells them he sees giant ants and little planes in the river. Graham sees the concrete bed

Then he turns too late and is crushed in the ant's mandibles.

of the dry Los Angeles River storm drain system, outside the hospital window. At one of the entrances to the 700 miles of underground tunnels, they find model airplanes belonging to two boys missing since morning, when their father's body was found with his arm torn off. By dusk martial law has been declared. The military has taken control of the streets. We sweep across the faces of the public as they hear the incredible warning about giant ants somewhere under the city. It is now nightfall at the storm drain entrance and the military is massed in jeeps and trucks to mount the search in teams with Graham, Petersen, and Pat. The boys' mother waits disconsolately nearby.

For the second time we go down into the ants' world. The tunnels are like an enormous ant nest we see into, as the jeeps drive further and further, maintaining radio contact. Petersen hears the two boys first and climbs through a connecting tunnel to where an ant is terrorizing the cowering boys. He radios out that the area has the same strong "brood odor" he remembers from the nest in New Mexico. Troops race to the area as Petersen lifts the second boy to safety in the tunnel. Then he turns too late and is crushed in the ant's mandibles. Petersen dies while Graham kneels beside him. Another attack of ants causes a tunnel collapse and Graham is cut off alone. In the last cliffhanger, the soldiers free enough rubble to save Graham, sparing at least one of the two lead actors.

In a dead end tunnel two princess ants are found, and Medford says they are in time. The soldiers' flamethrowers pour into the new nest. Graham speaks as the flames reflect up onto his face: "If these monsters got started as a result of the first atomic bomb in 1945, what about all the others that have been exploded since then?" Medford's solemn answer concludes the film: "When man entered the Atomic Age he opened a door to a new world. What we'll eventually find in that new world nobody can predict." In truth, the atom stalked the darkness of the country's theaters throughout the 50s. No one was safe, not even the masters of the horrific. Before the end of the decade Boris Karloff used an atomic reactor to revive the monster in FRANKENSTEIN '70. And Bela Lugosi starred in BRIDE OF THE ATOM.

Another attack of ants causes a tunnel collapse.

CREATURE FROM THE BLACK LAGOON

As the decade proceeded, sci-fi films grew more and more popular. Movie-goers couldn't seem to get enough and there was no monster too outlandish to try on the public. In the slather and dust it was often hard to tell one horror from the next, all goo and tendrils. They came and went, oozing, staggering, lurching their respective ways into film oblivion or the sleepy memory of TV syndication film libraries. When you consider the sheer numbers of 50s sci-fi films, little was truly memorable. But there was one figure who rose up out of the din to a kind of permanent greatness, who heads up the decade's sci-fi movie hall of fame as its single best known visage. He was merchandised like a celebrity screen idol: on posters, paperbacks, pencil erasers, figurines, lunch boxes, belt buckles, bars of soap, and best of all, beach towels. He was the entire ocean, all the seas' finny glory come to join us out of the deeps: CREATURE FROM THE BLACK LAGOON.

And it was all because of a costume, a now celebrated design concept that was carried out in unparalleled elaborateness and expense. No matter how you look at it, CREATURE FROM THE BLACK LAGOON is preeminently an extended opportunity to parade around the nightmare in scaly armor. The film is a miniature of a movie really, almost like the setting of a ring, there to accent and offer up something besides itself. The idea originated when producer William Alland wanted to do a film based on a South American legend of a half-man, half-fish creature, a sort of gilled missing link. Alland asked Bud Westmore, then head of makeup at Universal, for some drawings of a creature. By this time, Alland had some specific characteristics in mind: the creature should have gills, swim well, and yet walk like a man. Alland even suggested a rough model for the creature's body type, the Academy of Motion Pictures' award figurine, Oscar. Westmore gave the project to Milicent Patrick of his staff, whose xenomorph in IT CAME FROM OUTER SPACE had worked so handily. She had been the first woman animator at Walt Disney studios, was an actress as well as an artist/designer, and had even acted and done design work in the same films.

Actual construction of the monster was carried out by makeup artist Jack Kevan and artist/sculptor Chris Mueller. Mueller sculpted the head, and a complex series of molds were made of the exterior of the costume and actors' bodies. The costume was made of rubber, a foam latex best described as "rubber meringue," that was poured into the molds

Dr. Carlos Maia makes an incredible discovery: it is the hand again.

and then baked and cured. Curing the latex was so involved it required specially built ovens. A total of three costumes were built in eight and a half months. Reports of the cost of the suits ran from twelve to eighteen thousand dollars, heralded as the most expensive costume ever in a sci-fi/horror film, and certainly the most complicated. At one point the creature even had a tail — motorized, to augment its bestial quality. When it proved a hindrance swimming — even motorized — it was mercifully chopped off. The costume was considered innovative enough a departure to warrant a cover story in the May, 1954 issue of MECHANIX ILLUSTRATED.

The movie was another effort from what became a regular rotating production crew at Universal, prominently headed by Alland and director Jack Arnold. The early success of IT CAME FROM OUTER SPACE brought more sci-fi projects to the two, who worked together on four such projects, and altogether account for more than a dozen sci-fi movies. The credits for IT CAME FROM OUTER SPACE, CREATURE (and its sequels), and THIS ISLAND EARTH alone read like musical chairs, involving more than a dozen recurring names. Clifford Stein, originally Arnold's cameraman, worked on a number of the films and became head of Universal's special effects department. The films from the group came to be highly visible as a distinct body of work and highly regarded.

Like IT CAME FROM OUTER SPACE, CREATURE was filmed in 3-D. There was no mistaking the possibilities in combining the faddish 3-D film process with the 50s vogue in underwater photography. The darkened theater and shadowy waters of the Black Lagoon would join in mid-air, there where the creature swirled suspended above the audience. Two decades later, in the late 70s, as 3-D movies circulated on college and art theater circuits, IT CAME FROM OUTER SPACE and CREATURE FROM THE BLACK LAGOON were paired and re-released in a definitive 3-D package.

The underwater sequences in CREATURE FROM THE BLACK LAGOON were filmed on location in Silver Springs, Florida, chosen for the clarity of the water there. While scouting locations, director Arnold discovered a young swimmer, Ricou Browning, who had a remarkable capacity to hold his breath swimming underwater. He was hired to play the creature underwater, in a Ricou Browning-sized costume, while a second, larger actor, Ben Chapman, was recruited to fill the costume of the more menacing-sized, landgoing creature. Browning was able to perform all the swimming sequences by simply holding his breath and making trips off camera to an air hose. This simple arrangement also precluded air bubbles rising from the gilled creature. Almost an entire movie studio descended into the water for the atmospheric swimming scenes.

When we enter the world of the creature, we go back in time. The film begins with a standard

She is like a dream in a million years of sleep, a petal at the water's surface.

3-D explosion, which is explained as the creation of the Earth millions of years ago. The steamy seas give way to clawed tracks — guess whose? — leading out of the water and up onto a beach. We hear that man is still studying the record of life — fossils — millions of years later. We sweep in over a jungle canopy to men running at a camp site, somewhere in the Amazon forest. There, at a rock wall, Dr. Carlos Maia makes an incredible discovery: it is the hand again, the outstretched, clutching hand that keeps skipping from movie to movie like an icon, the gripping menace. Maia leaves to meet with a group of scientists; they study the hand on a table, mounted on a stand, the arched talons clawing up into the air even after a million years.

Dr. David Reed (Richard Carlson) is a marine biologist in the employ of Mark Williams (Richard Denning), imperious head of a research institute; Katy (Julia Adams) is Williams' assistant and both Reed and the creature's love interest. The party of researchers are studying the lungfish, a peculiar evolutionary bridge between marine and land life, and reverse metaphor of the "gill-man" creature. Reed connects their work with space research in terms of their studies of life at different pressures and in different atmospheres. He is careful to point out that the reaches of the sea are like space. If we are able to find out how life adapted here on Earth we might better adapt in outer space. While the air fills with scientific notions, at Maia's camp a live, working version of the hand appears out of the water. Something enters a tent and kills two men, the huge hand closing around each man's head as though it were a ball.

Williams, mindful of the value of publicity to his institute, proposes they join forces with Maia to retrieve the entire fossil. The party sails up a river to Maia's camp on a small, shabby vessel, the RITA, whose captain, Lucas, regales them with tales of prodigious Amazon jungle life, and centipedes a foot in length. As they approach the camp a hand protrudes grotesquely from the water; it is one of the dead men, calling card of the clawed hand. In the first moments at the camp the hand reaches from the water again, narrowly missing when it grabs for Katy's ankle. After a few days' fruitless digging, Williams' remonstrations lead to the party moving up the tributary to its source in the legended "Black Lagoon" that Lucas speaks of ominously. The RITA heads even further into the claustrophobic jungle tangles.

When the RITA reaches the lagoon the film is reduced to its essentials, the boat and the water. The tiny cast now acts out the drama reduced to the eerie stage of the surface of the water, stagnant, redolent with time. The surface tension of the water is like the unnatural evenness of the desert. Perhaps it has never moved. Or is always just about to move. Time stands still when Williams and Reed don scuba gear to enter the lagoon and come

The creature wraps around the pole like the winding serpent in Eden.

swimming out of the screen in the first dramatic underwater 3-D display. We are in the black water of history itself, traveling in time. And there in the warp of the lagoon is the creature, traveling up towards us. The creature sees Katy swimming at the surface of the lagoon. His face seems to trail with question. He swims beneath her mirroring her motions in a ballet of beauty and the beast, the oldest fairy tale. The creature courts in the water, he is drawn nearer. What he might be in a million years stirs in his bulky form. She is like a dream in a million years of sleep, a petal at the water's surface.

The drama becomes one of sheer survival as the scientists struggle with the creature underwater and first wound it with a speargun. He then comes aboard the boat in all his magnificent scales. He pulls up at the side of the boat wrapping his hand and arm around a pole, then wraps his leg around it, like the winding serpent in Eden, the first beast. He seizes one of the mates and kills him before he is driven back overboard. Then he kills one of the scientists and first tries to carry off Katy. Reed still manages to capture the creature using a native poison Lucas suggests that paralyzes fish. The creature's brooding face fills the screen peering up out of a bamboo cage suspended in water. Suddenly he is free again, attacking, then set afire with a lantern and fought off.

As the group is slowly decimated, they decide to simply make a break for it. Too late, they find the narrow mouth of the lagoon blocked by a tree moved there by the creature. They must go down into the water one last time to free the passage, and face the creature. In the underwater struggle Williams is killed. The creature carries Katy away to his underwater cave, which is complete with a startlingly bogus 3-D bat that buzzes Reed as he pursues them. The creature is about to dispatch Reed when Lucas and Maia arrive in the cave and open fire, driving the creature out the front of the cave to a beach. In the last scene, the four see the creature shamble towards the surf and enter the sea.

Box office response to the doings in the Black Lagoon cried out for more. Not even those bloody, bullet gouged holes in its chest could stop the creature from returning. His success was so great he starred in two sequels. In REVENGE OF THE CREATURE, released in 1955, a year after the original, he is captured in South America — with the aid of Lucas — and taken to an oceanarium in the U.S. The underwater studios of Marineland, Florida provided the location setting. The movie included swimming sequences in oceanarium tanks filled with exotic marine life, and one large turtle that liked to chew on the creature costume. During underwater scenes, a crew member had to be used to keep the turtle away from the creature. The ingredients of the story are familiar: an animal psychologist and lovely young ichthyologist (fish scientist) examine the mental capacity

The creature about to dispatch Reed in the cave.

of the creature. Some elements were more explicit than previous, as advertising suggested: "A woman's beauty the lure for his dangerous desires!" In the climax, the creature literally cuts in on the professor, crashing into a restaurant in glorious 3-D, abducting the fish scientist.

The third movie of the series, THE CREATURE WALKS AMONG US, did without 3-D and director Arnold, but made up for this with a kind of ultimate treatment of the creature. Captured a second time, the creature undergoes an emergency tracheotomy and becomes an air-breather. Redoing the fire scene from the original film, the creature suffers third-degree burns and loses his gills. Scientists' x-rays show lung formations which are activated by the operation, saving the creature from suffocation. As the creature acclimates to its lung activity it starts to change and become humanoid.

First the hands lose their finned webbing. Then the face: "The fire burned away the outer scales. There's a structure of human skin underneath it. Two separate coverings. The way he had lungs and gills." There is a genuinely gripping change in the creature, who has clothes sewn for him on the voyage to the expedition's headquarters in Sausalito, California. The idea of accelerating the evolution of the creature is attractive, and so is the new creature. It is too bad the drama of his passage to air-breather is so cluttered with the lead scientist's jealousy over his wife. Perhaps it was the decade moving on.

In the film's most dramatic moment, the creature steps out from the dark inside the back of a truck, clothed like a Frankenstein monster. Gone is the Devonian wonder. The face is dulled, the features rubbed off to a permanent, questioning blank. Its dazed docility makes it seem like a kind of robot. The researchers windily debate the creature's progress, whether he is the key to evolution and the answer to the question of man's destiny, "The stars or the jungle." Regrettably, the creature is little more than a reverse metaphor of the scientist's descent into rage and bloodshed. When he kills one of the hired hands in a struggle over his wife, he throws the body in with the caged creature. Invigorated by the violence, the creature kills the scientist and makes for the sea one last time. Jeff Morrow and Rex Reason, the scientists, had better roles the same year — 1956 — in Universal's major production, THIS ISLAND EARTH.

A common idea about 50s sci-fi films is that they were the horror movies of the 30s all over again, dressed up in timely scientisms. For all the trappings, the one theme common to most of the films was threat, a menace of some kind, that is, fright. There is a kind of horror hangover in the decade's sci-fi films, and it is no clearer than in the figure of the

REVENGE OF THE CREATURE: "A woman's beauty the lure for his dangerous desires!"

CREATURE FROM THE BLACK LAGOON. His cave lairs, his beast's longing for beauty, the dark, shadowy reaches of his world beneath the surface of the waters — all are characteristic of classic terror traditions that lead back past the beginnings of film into literature and folktales. He is, in fact, the one figure in sci-fi film who by common consent joined the highest ranks of dark cinema. Today the CREATURE FROM THE BLACK LAGOON is as readily recognized as Frankenstein, Dracula, and the Wolf Man, the fathers of 30s horror.

THE CREATURE WALKS AMONG US: He becomes an air-breather.

IT CAME FROM BENEATH THE SEA

The atom in the sea. Within a year of the Trinity atomic test and the two bombs dropped on Japan, there were two more nuclear explosions, in the South Pacific. "Operation Crossroads" took place at Bikini Atoll in the Marshall Islands, 2000 miles southwest of Hawaii. For each test a target fleet was assembled, nearly 200 damaged and captured vessels from the war. Three thousand goats and mice made a guinea pig crew for the ghost armada. A wing of automaton planes was launched and flown through the blast storm clouds. Test Able, July 1, 1946: an A-bomb was detonated in the air, several hundred feet above the ocean's surface. Test Baker, July 25: an A-bomb was detonated underwater. On November 1, 1952, Eniwetok in the Marshalls was the site of the first U.S. H-bomb test. On March 1, 1954, a second H-bomb explosion at Eniwetok inadvertently showered Japanese fishermen (and their vessel, the LUCKY DRAGON!) with radioactive coral dust.

That same year, the first atomic submarine was launched and commissioned, the U.S.S. NAUTILUS, named for Captain Nemo's submarine in the classic Jules Verne adventure, TWENTY THOUSAND LEAGUES UNDER THE SEA. The NAUTILUS was a joint project of the Navy and the Atomic Energy Commission. Nuclear research now reached from remote desert stretches to the silent depths of the seas. The NAUTILUS was commissioned in September, 1954, and put to sea for its first trials in January, 1955. In the first moments of IT CAME FROM BENEATH THE SEA — released in 1955 — a narrator's voice describes efforts towards the construction of the first atomic submarine. We see primitive drawings of the first submarines, molten ore pouring in heavy industrial manufacturing, and finally a submarine sliding into water. There is the classic shot of the deck of a diving submarine seen from its conning tower, the shot you've seen if you've ever seen any submarine movie. Water swirls over the steel-ridged deck and the vessel is gone beneath the surface, like a coin lost down a drain.

A very conventional submarine movie begins, about the maiden voyage of the country's first atomic sub, which has now established three new world records. It is the customary inside of a submarine with a journeyman military figure at the helm, Kenneth Tobey as Commander Pete Mathews. A radar man reports a shape tagging the ship, keeping pace with its movements. The strange form stalks the ship until the sub's motion is

There are tentacles everywhere, the ship rocks in the nest the arms make.

135

suddenly halted and radiation readings climb. The crew check the engines, the drive mechanism, the atomic reactor, but nothing is wrong. The sub is operating under full power but is held in check. Then the ship begins tossing and pitching, a tremendous shaking force grips the submarine like a toy in a hand. When the sub is abruptly freed it surfaces with traces of radioactivity and something fouled in the rear fins, a large chunk of peculiar rubbery material.

IT CAME FROM BENEATH THE SEA, Ray Harryhausen's second feature film, was the brainchild of producer Charles Schneer and began where BEAST FROM 20,000 FATHOMS left off. It resurrected half the original title of the first movie and was another beast on the loose story. Beginning with BEAST one riotous monstrosity after another tore across the screen: dinosaurs, insects, protozoa, claws, gila monsters, leeches. A truly memorable monster was hard to come by, and Schneer's inspiration was a good idea: he envisioned an octopus big enough to attack the Golden Gate Bridge in San Francisco. (An octopus had been considered as well at one point for BEAST.) It is not hard to understand the octopus as a screen villain. It is a perfect terror, a nightmare.

A brain out for a walk at the bottom of the sea. A mouth with arms, a hand with eight fingers. Sea spider, with poisonous, paralyzing saliva. A nest, a writhing ball of snakes. Medusa's head. Death's bonnet to tie around the neck. Each tentacle a nursery with rows of sucking mouths. It has no skeleton so it wafts in the water. It has three hearts. A thick, sharp beak like two talons. It is carnivorous. Squids, octopi, they definitely had their place in a certain kind of sea-going adventure. Possibly Schneer and Harryhausen knew of an obscure short story by sci-fi writer Arthur C. Clarke, "Big Game Hunt," about scientists who lure a gigantic squid alongside a yacht with electronic impulses. Certainly they knew about the original movie of TWENTY THOUSAND LEAGUES UNDER THE SEA, a silent feature made in 1916, and its giant squid, 40-feet long and operated by a diver hidden in its head. Even John Wayne fought it out with an octopus at the bottom of a pearl bed in WAKE OF THE RED WITCH, in the 40s.

The ambition and the accomplishment of IT CAME FROM BENEATH THE SEA are readily apparent when considered in relation to another fine sci-fi film of the day, the Walt Disney version of TWENTY THOUSAND LEAGUES, released in 1954. An enormous red squid that attacks the NAUTILUS is easily the most memorable element in the film. This full-size model weighed two tons and stretched 50 feet in length. It took teams of dozens of men to operate the sprawling apparatus with overhead wires, compressed air systems, and a remote electrical control panel. Scenes of the squid attacking the crew of the NAUTILUS called for a tank of water 90 by 165 feet, from 3- to 12-feet deep.

Arms pull up onto the steel piling, then the bulging hood of the head.

Harryhausen's octopus pulls a tramp freighter beneath the surface of the sea, mounts the Golden Gate, attacks San Francisco slinging its tentacles blocks down Market Street — and was just under two feet across its tentacles.

At Pearl Harbor, Mathews meets with two scientists about the strange material found in the submarine's fins, Drs. John Carter (Donald Curtis), the founder of analytical biology, and Lesley Joyce, a foremost authority on marine life. Mathews immediately begins to flirt with the alluring Dr. Joyce, actress Faith Domergue. She is an unusually present sex interest in the movie, veering between the two men at first, and then falling for the Navy commander. She even vamps a sailor mercilessly, bared shoulder, cigarette, and all, for information about a reported sighting of the octopus. After two weeks, the scientists say the substance is from a living creature, an octopus, but of a monstrously large size.

Screenwriter George Worthing Yates more or less redid the explanation of the giant ants in THEM, for Lesley's theory of the giant octopus. The octopus is not an atomic mutation itself, but is afoot because of nuclear explosions, and it is radioactive. One of the extraordinary creatures — long thought to exist by scientists, Lesley explains — has stirred from its depths at the ocean's floor. Contamination from H-bomb tests in the Marshall Islands drifted into the Mindanao Deep, a chasm in the sea bottom so deep it has never been explored. The octopus has become radioactive by feeding upon contaminated fish, and now "warns" prey off. It has risen to the surface in hunger and is roaming the shipping lanes of the North Pacific along the Japanese Current. Lesley concludes angrily when Navy authorities can't accept her theory.

Night at sea. A freighter makes its way in faint light. We see men at the ship's helm and sailors at railings. Then one points out across the waves to something unbelievable. A tentacle rises from the sea as though from nowhere and stands rigid. It makes a grotesque stalk against the dark sky, the suckers like flowers on a stem. Then the thick trunk sways and falls on the ship and another, the octopus engulfs the ship in its massive, wrapping arms. A wonder of animation and stop-motion photography, there are tentacles everywhere, the ship rocks in the nest the arms make, then it's gone like a spider with a fly. But six arms only, economy magic, a budget-wise six-tentacled model that only seems to have the proper number of tumultuous extremities.

This "sextopus" has come to be an integral part of the Harryhausen legend, perhaps the single most repeated anecdote about his films. More than two decades after the film's release, Harryhausen and Schneer could be seen interviewed on TV at sci-fi conventions, and still asked about the famous short-changed octopus. There's even been scholarly fan confusion over the number of tentacles the creature did have, five or

A tentacle shoots above the bridge and slams down crushing the automobile.

six. Harryhausen's own book, FILM FANTASY SCRAPBOOK, provides an authoritative answer, six. The "budget picture" nature of his early films — often lamented by Harryhausen — called for such masterful ingenuity; in this case, two tentacles less to construct and animate meant considerable savings in time and money.

Harryhausen designed and built the sexto/octopus of sponge rubber built up over steel armature skeletons for both the tentacles and head. The model was very small, something less than 24 inches stretched from tentacle tip to tip, with a head about the size of a baseball. Further octopus construction included lengths and tips of tentacles built on a larger scale, near three feet long, used in San Francisco scenes flailing in the streets and crashing into office fronts. A separate, detailed section of the head was also built, with an eye two inches in diameter, for the sequence of the scuba diver swimming past it at the film's climax.

Harryhausen's solitary animation work was particularly difficult with this film, involving a monster of such great size seen underwater. The bulk of the beast, and water resistance, would so slow its movements that animation proceeded by near infinitesimal increments. Water is also a difficult problem in model animation, because it is impossible to "miniaturize" its appearance. The octopus was never photographed in water in fact. Some footage of it was shot through water and distortion glasses that lent a "submerged" look; other scenes were optically combined with water footage. Finally, Harryhausen even took pains to optically add foam to scenes of the beast crashing in and out of the sea. To add to the creature's disagreeable appearance, the model was coated in glycerin and carefully photographed with at least one tentacle always in motion.

A group of survivors from the freighter is interviewed at a hospital. Lesley steams the story out of one of the sailors at last, in the parody vamp. The octopus is next seen off Astoria, Oregon. Mathews and the two scientists fly to the coastal area and see the monster at last, lashing its tentacles up onto a beach and dragging off a sheriff. Now the coastal waters of the Pacific are mined from the Arctic to Panama in "Operation Sea Beast." "Golden Gate Bridge Closed Tight," banners a newspaper headline. At the San Francisco Navy Yard Mathews and Lesley explain an experimental jet torpedo the sub will fire at the octopus; it will be exploded electronically after it is embedded in the beast. Reporters crowd around Lesley as she shows old drawings and illustrations of giant octopi sightings through the ages.

At the bridge, offshore mines start exploding. Then a tentacle again, at the base of the bridge structure. A second and third arm pull up onto the steel piling and then the bulging hood of the head. Carter races onto the bridge in a police car to throw a switch charging the

An arm rears from the bay and hauls a boxcar into the air like a plaything.

bridge electrically and shock the octopus loose. A tentacle shoots above the bridge and slams down crushing the automobile, as Carter stands at the electrical panel. Mathews drives another car out onto the bridge rescuing Carter, as the octopus tears a chunk out of the bridge, breaking the span.

The second-best known anecdote about the film involves efforts to film the Golden Gate Bridge and San Francisco sequences. To obtain official cooperation and approval to photograph landmarks, the film script was submitted to the city administration. When officials got to the sundering of the Golden Gate, they quickly denied the application and refused approval. It had something to do with public confidence in the bridge. The ingenious film company then resorted to newsreel and stock footage, and Harryhausen has also related how the camera crew rode back and forth across the bridge in the back of a bakery van, shooting background footage to be used in combination with a miniature Golden Gate Bridge.

Then the octopus appears dockside. An arm rears from the bay and hauls a boxcar into the air like a plaything. The bulbous sack of the head pulls up into view over the Embarcadero waterfront. Crowds pour through the streets as the tentacles tower in the sky. A helicopter falters in the air to avoid the arms swaying before it; one fills the screen through the copter window before it's struck out of the sky. Tentacles lash out down the streets and suck hold. The arms sway before the Ferry Building clock tower. Terrified crowds inside see elephantine, writhing trunks through the steel window latticing. The tentacles snake into office fronts and smash through restaurants. Squads of soldiers with flamethrowers advance on a tentacle at an intersection. It rears up and curls back from the streams of fire.

Mathews races to the sub after narrowly escaping a falling wall crushed by the octopus. Through binoculars, its arms are seen wrapped around the clock tower. The atomic sub fires the jet torpedo at last, but is clutched by the beast as the torpedo penetrates the side of its hood. The octopus lies beneath the wharfside holding the submarine like a small bar of soap. Mathews exclaims, "This is where we came in," and barks, "This is a personal matter," donning scuba gear. He swims to the octopus but an explosive he is carrying detonates, knocking him out. Carter goes out after him and swims before the gorged ball of the octopus' eye. It fills the screen like a planet as the tiny frogman moves past. Carter is able to fire a harpoon into a sensitive area between the beast's eyes, penetrating its brain. The sub is freed and Carter rescues Mathews. The octopus is then dispatched with an underwater explosion and all ends well, as Mathews, Lesley and Carter listen in a nightclub to a TV recital of the day's military efforts.

The head pulls up into view over the Embarcadero waterfront.

The Harryhausen animation genius progressed with each additional picture, and has continued to astonish audiences through the 70s. Harryhausen essentially continues to photograph miniature models, but his first two feature films were but the beginnings of a continuing refinement of animation systems. This first project with producer Schneer proved to be especially fortuitous for both men, as well as for the movie-going public. A very special bond formed between the two, and IT CAME FROM BENEATH THE SEA was the first of more than a dozen pictures made together over the next two decades. Following the octopus movie, the two made EARTH VERSUS THE FLYING SAUCERS, again with screenwriter Yates. Animation of a saucer attack on Washington, D. C. included the disintegration of buildings complete with individually wired tiny bricks.

Harryhausen's most acclaimed work came in JASON AND THE ARGONAUTS, with its famed sequence of three men dueling with seven skeletons. These scenes were filmed at a rate of thirteen film frames a day! Harryhausen's art has even kept pace with the vagaries of Hollywood stardom and fashion. In ONE MILLION YEARS B.C., he created a three-inch Raquel Welch for a pterodactyl to carry off. And the octopus? It went the way of most of Harryhausen's early models, evolving into other creatures as new film projects and new budget circumstances necessitated miniature sacrifices. First one tentacle and then another would become the tail of this dinosaur, or part of that monster, until the celebrated terror of San Francisco Bay was nothing but the forlorn baseball-sized head.

The arms sway before the Ferry Building clock tower.

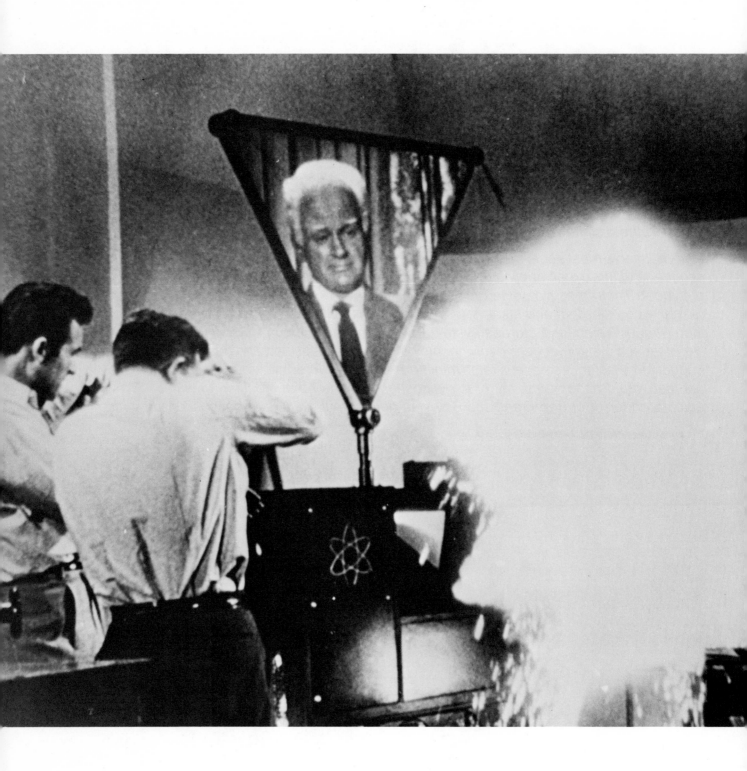

THIS ISLAND EARTH

Throughout the 50s, Universal studio did well with its sci-fi films, typically budget "B" features filmed in black and white. Movies like IT CAME FROM OUTER SPACE and CREATURE FROM THE BLACK LAGOON enjoyed particularly good returns, in part because they weren't very expensive. At one point the studio decided to vary the approach. With the mounting number of sci-fi pictures, competition had sharpened. Universal had the money, and felt the need, to try a more ambitious project. Producer William Alland assembled many of his regular sci-fi production crew members, but the direction they took was a departure for the studio: a color spectacular of warfare in deep space, a drama sweeping from a secret scientific community in the U.S. to an exotic extraterrestrial landscape an unimaginable distance from Earth. THIS ISLAND EARTH, released in 1955, was the most elaborate sci-fi production to come out of Universal in the 50s.

The original story, by Raymond F. Jones, was serialized in 1952 in THRILLING WONDER STORIES. In 1953 it was published revised as a novel by a major publisher of sci-fi in the early 50s, Shasta Publishers of Chicago. Jones' story was a timely blend of ideas and elements, from its title to the motivation of its characters. An alien civilization, locked in mortal combat with a second alien force, has manufacturing plants located on Earth, employing unknowning humans. Jones likens the situation to the Pacific in World War II: "You saw these primitive peoples sometimes employed or pressed into service by one side or the other. On the islands of your seas they build airfields for you; they sometimes cleared jungles and helped lay airstrips. They had no comprehension of the vast purpose to which they were contributing a meager part . . . . Earthmen, like the islanders of their own seas when Earth's wars swirled around them, had no capacity for understanding the power and depth of the forces involved."

The story echoes World War II — and its ending — in another way. The alien emissaries are first able to lure a human scientist to join their effort by appealing to his revulsion over what happened with atomic power: "It has undoubtedly occurred to you, as to all thinking people of your day, that the scientists have done a particularly abominable job of dispensing the tools they have devised. Like careless and indifferent workmen they have tossed the products of their craft to gibbering apes and baboons. The results have been disastrous, to say the least. We believe the world could better utilize the productions of

Exeter smiles faintly and fires a ray from the tips of the interociter.

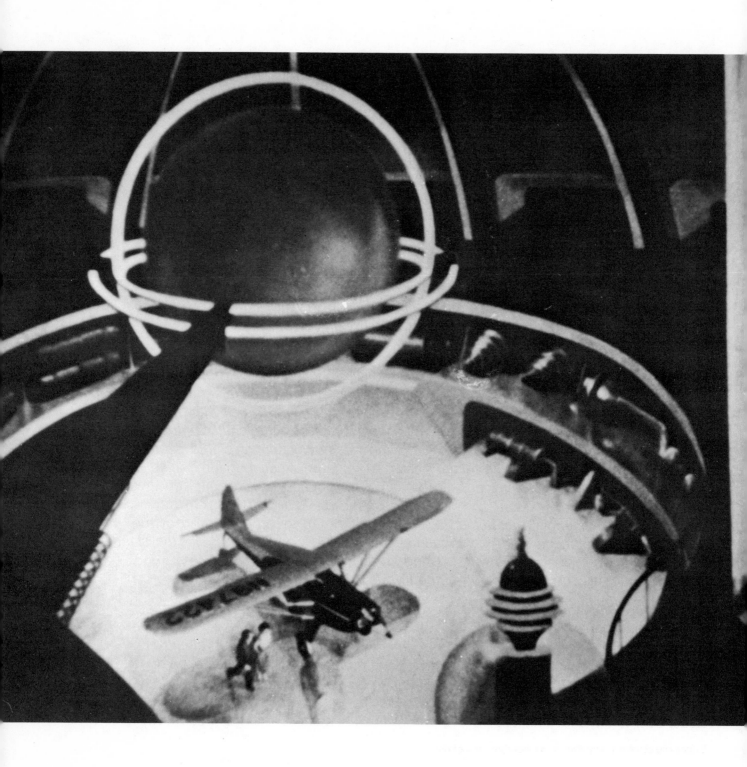

science if scientists themselves placed some restriction on the use of their talents."
The aliens use an organization, the "Peace Engineers," to cover their activities. Cal Meachum, the scientist, thinks: "Peace Engineers! They knew that half the scientists of the country were sick at heart after the last war because of what had happened through the discoveries of science." Jones' gloss of the Pandora's box nature of nuclear science reflected a grave concern early in the decade.

Jones' biggest idea in the novel regards science — technology — and overreliance on it. Meachum is at first almost overwhelmed by the advances of the alien science: "This technology — it's like breathing pure oxygen." In the lofty atmosphere of the research community glowing electronic tubes are "like candles of some ritual to the gods of science." Meachum resists the seduction of the alien technology though, and is able to offer this insight into the war predicament: the aliens' battle plans are entirely predictable, because they are entirely computer derived and ordained, hence orderly. It is precisely the aliens' braininess that defeats them. Most of these ideas don't get into the film, THIS ISLAND EARTH, but a certain braininess does.

Meachum, a researcher at Ryberg Electronics in Los Angeles, is on a return flight from a conference in Washington, D.C. in a sleek Lockheed F-80 Shooting Star. Near his landing strip, the jet flames out — loses its propulsive power — and he loses control of the plane. As it falls, it is enveloped by a green glow and a pulsing hum. The plane is guided to earth and landed safely, to the puzzlement of Meachum and his assistant, Joe Wilson. In his lab, Meachum finds he has been mysteriously sent some peculiar electronic parts; then an even more peculiar parts catalogue arrives, with untearable metal pages. The manual describes equipment and a technology that stagger Meachum. His scientific curiosity impels him further, and he is soon assembling a piece of equipment, an "interociter." When it is completed, the figure of a man appears on its strange, triangular video screen.

The construction of the machine was an I.Q. test for Meachum, an entrance examination of sorts. The man in the interociter is Exeter, leader of the aliens (mercifully not Jorgasnovara, "The Engineer," of the novel). He invites Meachum to join an exclusive research community of scientists from all over the world. Meachum's scientific questing plays into the hands of the aliens. Exeter says as much, explaining he knew Meachum would find their invitation irresistible. It is as if science is the tempter, the snake in the garden. Meachum wants to know more and so he can be led. His brain gets him in over his head, so to speak.

And Exeter is a brainy fellow himself. Actor Jeff Morrow provides a perfect forehead to begin

Inside the saucer, Cal and Ruth are led from the plane.

with, and makeup the rest of a wonderfully articulated alien cranium-ness. Exeter, his assistant/henchman Brack, the Monitor, all are classics of the overdeveloped brain image of aliens, complete with foreheads like windshields. When Meachum secretly talks with two other scientists about the group, they even go over drawings of the aliens' unusual forehead development. Brain concern extends to the aliens' thought transformer, a behavior control machine that eliminates the will. Actor Rex Reason (Meachum) even provides an unintentional tag line for the movie's preoccupation with his name: "King Reason."

The interociter is another important image and element in the movie. It really deserves co-star status, as it dominates nearly the first half of the film. Jones' original description of its cube-shaped video screen was tailored some, lest the audience be reminded of TV, hence the unusual triangular screen. The interociter is a means of communication, and as Exeter demonstrates early in the film, it is also a weapon. At the conclusion of their first "meeting," Exeter smiles faintly and fires a ray from the tips of the screen, vaporizing the parts catalogue. Then the interociter self-destructs, leaving only a whisper of smoke and dust. Meachum accepts the invitation to take a mysterious plane ride. Entering an empty plane with a blacked-out cockpit, he finds a single armchair and a small interociter piloting the craft.

The research facility is an antebellum mansion and estate located somewhere in Georgia. Meachum is met by glamourous Dr. Ruth Adams, sci-fi familiar Faith Domergue. Meachum claims to know Ruth and recalls their swimming together in a lake five years earlier. She insists not, mysteriously. At the mansion, Meachum meets the "head" man, Exeter, and takes an interociter tour of the grounds. In a wonderful scene, they sit before Exeter's interociter, in armchairs on either side of the screen, looking up at the image of another tiny interociter on the screen of the first one.

Exeter's few blithe remarks about seeking world peace do not convince Meachum. He confronts Ruth and a second scientist, Steve Carlton, about his questions, and they take him into their confidence (Ruth admitting yes, they were old friends). The pair have documentation and detailed drawings of the installation and like Meachum are concerned that the entire nature of the project is the generation of new sources of atomic energy. They plan to leave before being put under one of Exeter's "sunlamps," the thought transformers, that Steve says perform something like a lobotomy.

Exeter receives word to leave the Earth and return to the home planet as the scientists try to escape. Brack demonstrates another function of the interociter as the three race across the countryside in a paneled station wagon. Great bolts of the green ray fire

The saucer soars away from Earth bound for Metaluna.

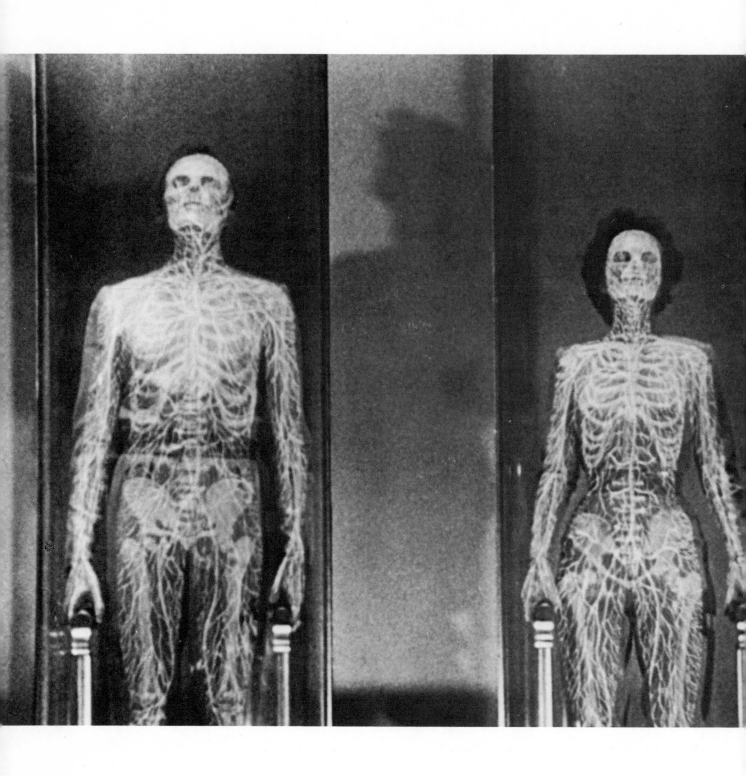

down on either side of the speeding auto. Steve drops Cal and Ruth and races on, drawing the fire of the interociter. The station wagon is then hit and vaporized, but Cal and Ruth are safe. They've even wound up back together swimming, having fallen into a pond. They run to a small airfield as an enormous saucer rises from behind a hilltop at the end of the runway. Cal pilots the plan aloft, but to no avail. The giant saucer hovers over the plane and projects the green ray again, a soft humming glow this time, that slowly hauls the plane up like a toy. Inside the saucer, Cal and Ruth are led from the plane as it soars away from the Earth.

Exeter explains they are bound for Metaluna, his home planet. The tide of war with the Zahgons has turned against his civilization, and they must return with the research effort to join the Metalunan forces. Exeter says it is time for all "conversions," necessary to leave the Earth's atmosphere and enter Metaluna's. The planet's atmosphere is dense, like the bottom of the oceans on Earth. Cal and Ruth mount a platform and stand in place while large transparent tubes descend over them, their hands magnetically gripped at their sides. As the eerie ceremony proceeds, Cal — ever human — wisecracks, "I feel like a new toothbrush." The scene glows with incandescent colors in an animated movie x-ray of their bodies. The saucer approaches the planet and Exeter explains about the ionized layer, a Metalunan protective forcefield that is now faltering for lack of uranium — the atomic power they need in enormous quantities to run the ion screen. Their mission on Earth was to accelerate research on the transference of elements into nuclear fuels.

The surface of the planet is a charred, steaming waste of craters, volcanoes, and explosions. War with the Zahgons has gone on so long, the entire Metalunan civilization has been forced underground. During the landing, Zahgon rockets relentlessly attack, diving towards the planet and releasing meteors guided down like missiles. The saucer fires and disintegrates a meteor hurled towards it, then glides down through a yawning crater opening into the vaulted chamber of the Metalunan capital city. There is a foreboding grandeur imposed over everything by the towering pitted ceiling of what was once the planet's surface. The sweeping aerial causeways and rising towers make a surreal landscape. The ambiguous forms of the city and features on the horizon recall the drippy objects in Dali's paintings and the landscapes of Yves Tanguy. The scene is especially like the 50s paintings of artist Richard Powers, who illustrated the covers of dozens of popular sci-fi paperback books.

Producer Alland supervised the special effects in the film, with his acclaimed talent for getting the most for the money. A 110-foot long miniature of the Metalunan surface and capital city was constructed. An elaborate overhead wire and track assembly ran the

Changing atmospheres in the conversion tubes: "I feel like a new toothbrush."

Metalunan saucer and Zahgon rockets. The saucer, largest of the ship models, was built out of aluminum and weighed some 18 pounds. Flaming meteors were plaster and magnesium packets that slid down wires to small gasoline explosions on the miniature landscape.

Exeter and the two humans descend from the docked saucer in a transparent shaft. They take a surface car across the devastated city to the building of the Monitor, the supreme head of the Metaluna civilization. The Monitor — Douglas Spencer, reporter "Scotty" in THE THING — is seated before a large model of an atom that he operates as some kind of instrument. He tells Exeter that relocation to Earth will be necessary. Cal and Ruth remonstrate about the takeover of the planet, but the Monitor threatens to change every brain on Earth if necessary. Exeter is commanded to take the humans to the thought transference chambers, but before he is able to carry out the order, a direct hit by a meteor on the building kills the Monitor and collapses the entire Metalunan defense system. Exeter realizes his planet is doomed and races with the humans to the saucer, to save them.

Suddenly a Metalunan mutant blocks the way into the saucer port. Exeter says the slave beasts were developed by their science to serve as manual laborers. Brains again, the swollen blue lobes and gorged red arteries of the hideous mutant, an unpleasant concoction of humanoid and insect features. The cranium-less brute is an inspired horror, a notable addition to the sci-fi movie brain bank. Ever since Frankenstein's monster went wrong, the brain has been a staple of horror/sci-fi films. There have been three versions of the Curt Siodmak novel, DONOVAN'S BRAIN, wherein a disembodied brain telephathically controls a scientist keeping it alive. In BRAIN FROM PLANET AROUS, large flying alien brains enter and control humans. FIEND WITHOUT A FACE featured a clump of "materialized thought" that sucks brains out of its victims' necks. And BRAINIAC (a Mexican film) was about another brain sucker.

The scene bears the handiwork of several Universal staffers. The mutant design and Metalunan costumes were by Milicent Patrick; construction of the monster was carried out by Jack Kevan, Chris Mueller, and Robert Hickman. The mutant was played by a Universal stuntman, Eddie Parker, equally versed in studio productions; he had previously played such Universal favorites as the Wolfman, Mummy, Mr. Hyde, and Frankenstein monster.

Exeter orders the mutant guarding the saucer, "Stand back. I command you stand back." But the mutant has been wounded in the attack and is disordered. It lunges and

The three tiny figures race to the saucer to escape the doomed planet.

THIS ISLAND EARTH 156

stabs Exeter with its hooked claw-hand. Cal literally beats on its brains with a wrench and rescues Exeter. Unbeknownst to the three, the bloodied mutant crawls on board the ship at the last moment. The struggle with the mutant aboard the saucer provides the last moments of threat and terror in the film. The mutant enters the control room while the three are in the conversion tubes and chases Ruth around when her tube rises first, before it collapses dead. It has that same peculiar Metalunan property of vaporizing into nothing but a greenish wisp.

Exeter is mortally wounded but is able to pilot the ship back to Earth. The saucer lowers the plane with the green ray and then crashes into the sea. Exeter's return of Cal and Ruth is characteristic of his nobility and magnanimous behavior throughout the adventure. First with Brack, then with the Monitor, Exeter argues against using the thought transformers on the humans. As the saucer hurtles into space leaving Metaluna behind, the three watch the planet become one cataclysmic nuclear explosion. Exeter is able to rise philosophically to speculation that Metaluna will become a glowing sun and warm another planet. His genteel and selfless manner recalls another alien emissary in a saucer, Klaatu in DAY THE EARTH STOOD STILL. Both are notable exceptions in the movie canon of visiting aliens. Both have a vision that outstrips humankind's. They see a greater whole of things, the connectedness of galaxies. Exeter's universal empathy is a sci-fi expression of the famous line of poetry, "No man is an island."

Suddenly a Metalunan mutant blocks the way into the saucer port.

FORBIDDEN PLANET

Shakespeare, Freud, and money. When MGM belatedly decided to enter the sci-fi movie derby, the resulting project was a mix of elements unlike any previous film. FORBIDDEN PLANET was loosely based on THE TEMPEST, the last play of the great English poet and playwright, William Shakespeare, and also included a good portion of psychology from the father of psychoanalysis, Sigmund Freud. To make the movie even more unlike standard sci-fi fare, MGM gave FORBIDDEN PLANET an unprecedented "A" picture budget of nearly two million dollars. The studio, mindful of its reputation in the 50s, was determined to provide a glittering counterpoint to the budget sci-fi films crowding the screen. FORBIDDEN PLANET, released in 1956, was a magnificent display of production virtuosity; its opulence alone would insure its standing in any survey of the decade's movie science fiction.

In 1954, artist and veteran special effects man Irving Block took an original story, "Fatal Planet," to MGM. A. Arnold Gillespie, whose career spanned some 600 films and two Oscars, oversaw production as MGM's head of special effects, and also contributed sketches and drawings, including Robby the robot. Bob Kinoshita did design work on the space cruiser interior as well as the startling Krell underground complex. Matthew Yuricich painted the Krell interiors. The gloss and polish of the production was such that for years costumes, props, and even sets from FORBIDDEN PLANET turned up in other movies and TV shows. The film was also nominated for an Oscar for special effects.

Even MGM executive Dore Schary was involved in the project. He had been approached by two musicians, Louis and Bebe Barron, with some experimental electronic music. Schary, intrigued by the strange sounds, imagined them together with FORBIDDEN PLANET and hired the Barrons. Their work was so innovative studio legal minds researched possible patent infringements. To ward off the musicians' union, the score was referred to as electronic "tonalities," Schary's own inspiration. The 25 minutes of atonal pings and whinings constituted the first entirely electronic musical score for a movie, using only the sounds of electric circuitry, and no musical instruments.

The sumptuousness of the film was a fitting match for the stature of its ideas. Shakespeare's TEMPEST is a familiar heading in most historical surveys of science fiction literature. In the tarot of science fiction the scientist is the magician, the wonder worker,

United Planets cruiser C57D landing on distant Altair-4.

159

the alchemist. The central figure in THE TEMPEST is Prospero, a magician in exile with his daughter, Miranda, on a remote island. He has devoted the years of their seclusion to study and the refinement of his powers. Ariel, Prospero's spirit servant, performs his master's magic and was freed from a tree by Prospero, where he had been imprisoned by the former master of the island, a witch, Sycorax. The witch also left a son, Caliban, who is a dark, bestial figure. Prospero's magic draws a passing ship to the island. The party of men includes the conspirators who set Prospero adrift twelve years earlier, so the magician and his servant bedevil the party of men with tricks, and a pack of spirit dogs that pursues them. Ferdinand, son of one of the consipirators, falls in love with Miranda, and is set to menial tasks that hinder the romance. In the end, all is put right. The couple are to be married, and Prospero declares he will put away his magic and use it no more.

As FORBIDDEN PLANET begins, we are propelled forward in time more than three hundred years, to the 23rd century. A ship from Earth is a year into its flight in deep space, bound for a distant planet, Altair-4, and an Earth colony there that has not been heard from in twenty years. United Planets cruiser C57D is a classic flying saucer; by the mid 50s humans had their own saucers for interplanetary flight. Commander J.J. Adams (Leslie Neilsen) and members of the crew wonder about the fate of the colony when a voice radios the ship as it draws near the planet. It is Edward Morbius, one of the original party, who tries to dissuade Adams from landing. He finally says, "I warn you that I cannot be answerable for the safety of your ship or your crew."

Adams reads from the roster of the colony that Morbius is a philologist, or scientist of languages, a linguist. Morbius' science is an ultimate intellectual challenge, the structure of language and consciousness itself. Morbius' "atoms" — words — constitute the very fabric of existence, self-consciousness. The word "philology" comes from Greek meaning loving reason or learning, and loving words. Morbius' love of "mind" makes him a scientist par excellence; in the drama of his tinkering with his own mind he becomes a magician, a master of the invocative properties of words and thought.

Dauntless, and dutiful, Adams brings the saucer across the surface of the planet — a 350-foot wide painted cyclorama — and lands. The sequence of the saucer landing employed animation footage from MGM cartoonists, as well as three different sized models of the saucer, ranging down from some six feet in diameter; the smallest model, less than two feet across, was used in space flight sequences. The only full-size construction on the saucer exterior was the bottom and ladder. All other external features of the ship were added to footage using paintings.

Robby the robot greets the cautious Earthmen.

In the grainy expanse of desert reds and oranges, jagged spires and crags rise up. The sky is green. There are two moons. Almost immediately, a thin trail of dust appears near the horizon, streaking towards the ship. It is Morbius' Ariel, Robby the robot. The robot addresses the crew in articulate English and bids Adams and two others aboard the surface car for a call on the philologist. At lunch, Moribus demonstrates some of Robby's capabilities and has him molecularly manufacture food. Morbius then has Robby point a blaster pistol at the three men and commands him to fire, his way of illustrating that the programmed robot may not harm a human.

Robby was a great success with the public and became another icon of 50s sci-fi. The robot was a costume, really, another "suit" worn by a person, in this instance two persons who traded off the difficult job of ambulating Robby; the seven foot plastic shell and internal workings weighed a hundred pounds, including seven working motors and various inside controls. An off-camera extension cable connected Robby to a power source; for scenes when the cable would show, he was fitted with motorcycle batteries. Robby's voice was Marvin Miller, whose purring tones were familiar to viewers of the 50s TV series, THE MILLIONAIRE. The occasional bursts and flurries of energy patterns in Robby's transparent head were animation footage combined with live action.

It is a particularly fateful "trick" Morbius has Robby perform. When Robby points the blaster at the Earthmen, it is a version of the ultimate drama in the movie, the marshaling of the Krell power against the visitors. Morbius also now first speaks of the fate of the colony. "Some dark, terrible, incomprehensible force" began to ravage the settlement, Morbius tells them; settlers were torn limb from limb. When a vote was taken to return to Earth, only he and his wife wanted to stay. As the rocket BELLEROPHON lifted from the planet with three last colonists, it was vaporized. A few months later Morbius' wife died. Now, he says, there are no others. Walter Pidgeon as Morbius lent the film a name presence, and brought an appropriate sobriety to the role. His manner is foreboding, his mood austere, he even dresses in black. Morbius is all concentration, momentarily distracted by the Earthmen.

No sooner has Morbius announced there are no other colonists, than his daughter, Altaira, appears. She enchants the men, and the crew at the saucer, who are able to gawk via Adams' small video transmitter; wolf whistles and exclamations burst from the device. The crew's reaction to Altaira is played broadly, for comic relief, in a parody of a crew of sailors a year at sea. Altaira's gushing entrance line — "What beautiful men!" — is a 50s paraphrase of Miranda's famous greeting: "O, wonder! How many goodly creatures are there here! How beauteous mankind is! O brave new world that has such people

"Prepare your minds for a new scale of scientific values, gentlemen."

in't!" Anne Francis' short hems and naiveté undo the men altogether. First Adams has to ward off a crewmember who experiments with kissing with Altaira, then he falls for her himself. Altaira's world is Edenic, as is her camaraderie with the wild beasts in it. She has a pet tiger that is moved to violence only after Adams kisses her.

The intrigue proceeds when someone or something enters the saucer and sabotages radio transmission equipment. Adams and Ostrow (Warren Stevens), the medical officer, go to speak with Morbius, who tells them the first secret of the planet, the story of the Krell civilization. The Krell were the first inhabitants of Altair-4, a race of superbeings that had evolved to supreme accomplishments. Morbius says they dreamed of a civilization without instrumentality, freed from dependence on material objects, total mind over matter. They were on the brink of some crowning achievement when, in a single night, the civilization was destroyed in some mysterious upheavel, that wiped the Krell from the planet. Morbius leads the two Earthmen down an underground corridor to a Krell laboratory, replete with gauges and controls.

Morbius shows Adams and Ostrow the "plastic educator," a toy for Krell young. The first time he tried it the shock knocked him unconscious but permanently doubled his intellectual capacity. For two decades he has eked his way into the Krell civilization, using the plastic educator and deciphering the Krell language. He tells them he was able to build Robby using Krell technology. In a demonstration of the plastic educator, Morbius sits in a headset and conjures a hologram-like image of Altaira. He then leads the men from the lab to a shuttle car with the pregnant words, "Prepare your minds for a new scale of scientific values, gentlemen." The three descend miles into the planet, into the awesome majesty of the Krell machinery complex.

A good deal of the Krell interiors were paintings and animation footage, but the ventilator shaft was a miniature (!) model, 30-feet long and 10-feet across at the top, photographed horizontally. The visual effect is stunning as the camera seems to wheel in mid-air over the shaft and the men peer down an infinite distance where bolts of electricity rise and fall. Morbius says there are 400 such shafts, extending 20 miles up and 20 miles down inside the planet. They walk through the Krell power complex, three dots lost in the towering, labyrinthine chambers, and Morbius describes thermal nuclear reactors miles below in the center of the planet; he says the furnace has the power of an exploding planetary system. The purpose of the entire complex is a mystery Morbius has not yet solved. When we go down into the machineworks it is like going inside the mind of the planet. The machines are a vast, inpenetrable dream, some purpose as yet unawakened:

An infinite distance where bolts of electricity rise and fall.

"It's a thinking machine. For two thousand centuries it has waited patiently here tuning and lubricating itself, replacing worn parts."

At the saucer, the invisible force enters the ship and murders a crewman (Engineer Alonzo Quinn, named for Shakespeare's character Alonso). Word reaches Adams as he argues with Morbius about his monopolizing the Krell knowledge. A cast is taken of a print left by the mysterious beast: "This thing runs counter to every known law of adaptive evolution. Anywhere in the galaxy this is a nightmare." The crew sets up an electronic field around the saucer and mounts a force cannon. Another night brings a confrontation with the beast, seen for the first and only time. The invisible presence shows up in outline as the field is broken. Electricity flies up around it and then the fire of the crew's blasters and cannon. The broken red form of the beast flails and howls through the electric field. It reaches and clutches a crewman, hurling him through the air.

Originally, the beast was conceptualized as entirely invisible. Joshua Meador, on loan from the Walt Disney studios, animated what we do see of the creature. Its ambiguous outlines have given rise to a variety of impressions. It has been described as a cross between the MGM lion logo and a Japanese sumo wrestler, and a cross between a sabre-toothed tiger and the Warner Bros. cartoon character, Yosemite Sam. It also looks very much like a late 70s Warner Bros. cartoon character, the Tasmanian Devil.

After the attack, Adams and Ostrow decide one of them has to get into Morbius' lab and use the plastic educator to solve the mystery before the party is doomed. At the house, Altaira greets them. Ostrow runs ahead to the lab while Adams tells Altaira they must leave the planet. Robby then enters carrying Ostrow in his arms. He has solved the Krell mystery and the mystery of the beast, but it costs him his life. With a burn on his forehead where the headpiece fit, Ostrow gasps to Adams: "You ought to see my new brain. The Krell had completed the project. The big machine. No instrumentality. True creation. But the Krell forgot one thing. Monsters. Monsters from the Id." He collapses dead as Morbius enters.

Adams tells him they are all leaving, including Altaira, but Morbius refuses to believe him. He then asks Morbius what the "Id" is. Morbius replies, "An obsolete term, I'm afraid, once used to describe the elementary basis of the subconscious mind." The "Id," a term from Freud's theory of the structure of mental functioning, was the unconscious repository of animal instincts in humans. It constituted the sexual, the primitive, the violent aspects of human nature, ever warring with man's conscious, socialized self. Adams suddenly understands what happened to the Krell and tells Morbius. The Krell had succeeded in their quest for pure thought control, the machines did in fact carry out

"Anywhere in the galaxy this is a nightmare."

their every desire, to a fault. The energy potential of the machines was activated by the impulses of the Krells' minds, conscious and unconscious. "The beast. The mindless primitive. Even the Krell must have evolved from that beginning. And so those mindless beasts of the subconscious had access to a machine that could never be shut down." Morbius' saddened reply shows he finally understands: "My poor Krell."

But Morbius hesitates before the last secret of the planet. Adams reminds him, "The last Krell died two thousand centuries ago." Morbius, the adept, the initiate into the Krell mysteries, has been transformed into the new Krell. The monster rages outside the house as Adams tells Morbius the beast is him, his subconscious mind made strong enough to activate the machines and conjure up the monster. It was Morbius' unconscious mind that ravaged the BELLEROPHON party when the colonists wanted to return to Earth: "You sent your secret Id out to murder them." Adams says the same thing is happening again because of Altaira, making clear the underlying element of incestuous jealousy: "You're whistling up your monster again to punish her for disloyalty and disobedience."

The three run to Morbius' lab to cower behind 23 inches of impregnable Krell metal, but the door begins to slowly melt, progressing through a series of withering colors to blistering white. Adams beseeches Morbius to face the truth and repudiate the beast at the door. Finally, Morbius blurts out: "Then it's right. It must be. It must be me." Morbius is the mad scientist, the technologist consumed by the machine. He is Jekyll and Hyde, the doctor transformed by a fateful draught, knowledge. It is brain hubris. It is also the era's disquieting misgivings about science again, dressed up in psychology and the poetry of human drama. Morbius cries out before the door, "Stop! I deny you! I give you up!"

When a broken Morbius collapses, the force abates. He directs Adams to throw a switch that begins an unstoppable chain reaction in the Krell furnace. The saucer must be a hundred million miles away in 24 hours, when the planet will explode. Morbius remains on Altair-4, mortally wounded by the drama his mind played out. The wedding of Adams and Altaira aboard the saucer was filmed, bringing things to a close as Shakespeare did, but the sequence was cut from the film. FORBIDDEN PLANET is finally not THE TEMPEST. This Prospero must die to put things right; he gives up his magic by giving up his life. Prospero was Caliban, the murderous offspring of a race of Sycorax witches — the Krell magicians. In FORBIDDEN PLANET we go deep into space only to confront what is deepest in ourselves, secret impulses and desires we dare not be reminded of. The sophistication of the idea was remarkable for the times: for a threat, the film offers up a mirror.

Morbius cries out before the door, "Stop! I deny you! I give you up!"

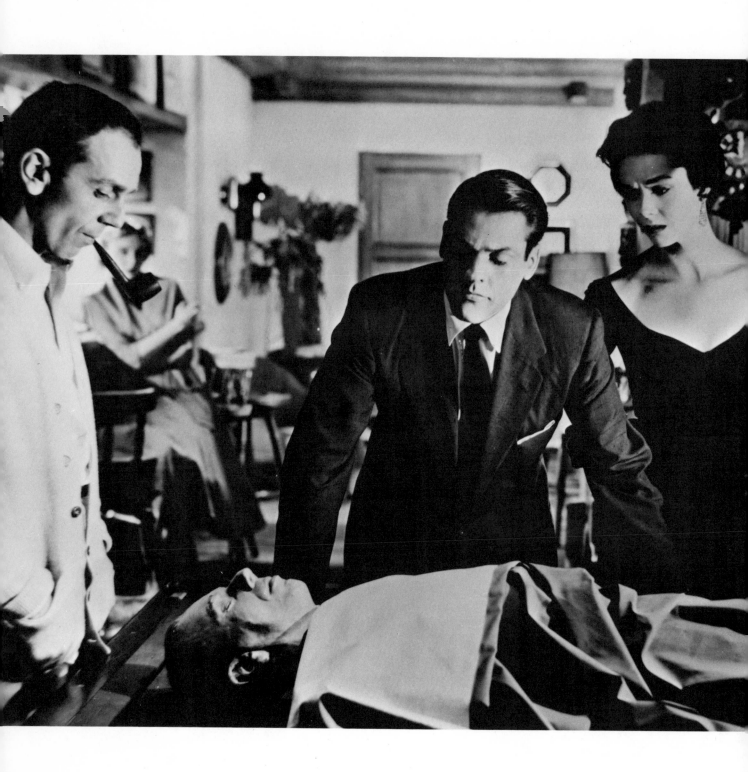

INVASION OF THE BODY SNATCHERS

Late in the fall of 1978, the WASHINGTON POST wire service carried a news story headlined, "Plan to Bury Radioactive Wastes in N.M. Proceeds." The article began, "The Energy Department intends to press ahead with a plan to bury radioactive wastes in a saltbed near Carlsbad, N.M., a department official said. The controversial experiment, if successful, could form the basis for a national program of nuclear waste disposal. Officials were 'optimistic that we can bury our first nuclear wastes in New Mexico by 1985 or 1986.'" The Carlsbad area lies in the southern extreme of the state, near the border with Texas, some 300 miles southeast of the site of the first atom bomb test in 1945. After three decades, the atom comes full circle and heads home to the old neighborhood. And late in the fall of 1978, newspapers carried the first advertisements for United Artists' heavily-promoted new film, INVASION OF THE BODY SNATCHERS, a remake of the original classic of 1956. Full circle.

Jack Finney's story, "The Body Snatchers," was serialized in 1954 in COLLIER'S magazine and a year later published in a lengthened version as a novel. The Daniel Mainwaring screenplay draws considerably from the novel, including particular scenes and even dialogue. Allied Artists added a sci-fi title prefix to the film and promoted it like another of its budget sci-fi features, but it was in fact very much unlike standard 50s sci-fi offerings. Director Don Siegel wanted to call the movie SLEEP NO MORE. Author Finney later said the work was "fantasy fiction," with no science to it at all. Though its menace did come from the sky, the film was a startling departure for the era, an exploration of menace and terror in the everyday surface of life. In the film's almost documentary approach, the landscape is familiar, authentic, recognizable like the back of a hand.

The story and director Siegel's approach were both explicit. INVASION OF THE BODY SNATCHERS is set in a small California town peopled by ordinary citizens coming and going in the most ordinary manner. The film was shot in 19 days using streets and homes in Hollywood neighborhoods for location settings, part of the movie's resolute realism. The non-star cast of supporting and character actors added to the calculated realism of the production. Siegel intentionally eschewed special effects in the film. He had worked in special effects for several years, and particularly wanted to avoid such emphasis in the film. In an era of space hardware and spectacular visual effects,

A strange, imprecise replica of a man, "Like the first impression of a coin."

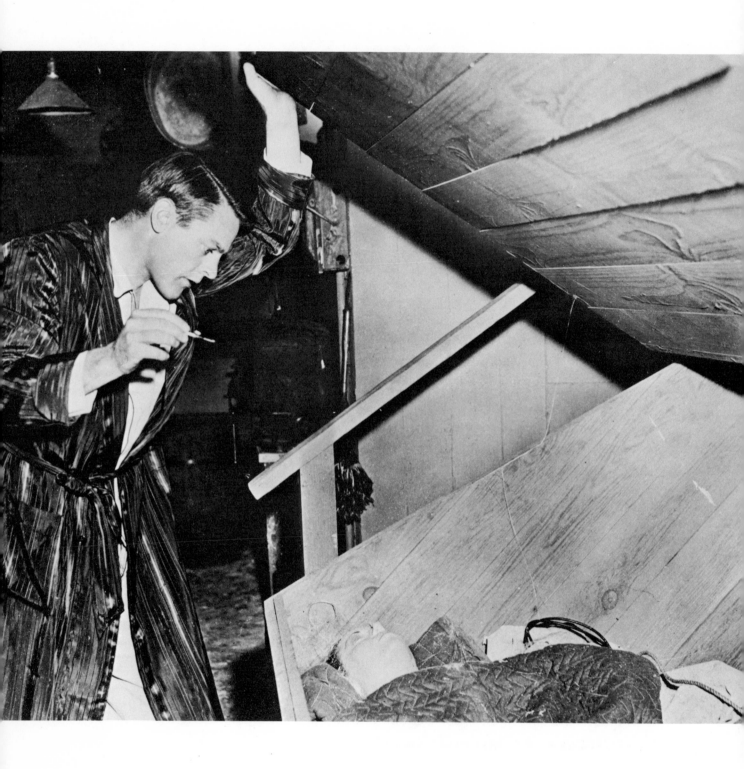

Siegel was determined that BODY SNATCHERS be different in this regard, and stress instead character development and the story line. INVASION OF THE BODY SNATCHERS is about states of mind; it is psychological science fiction. The strangest things in the movie happen inside people's heads, hidden behind seeming normality.

At the beginning of the film, a psychiatrist is speaking with a man who was picked up raving deliriously in the middle of a crowded freeway. The disheveled, agitated character is Dr. Miles Bennell (Kevin McCarthy), a medical practitioner himself from nearby Santa Mira, a small community located in the hilly areas of Marin County, across the Golden Gate Bridge from San Francisco. As Bennell begins his story, the scene dissolves to a train pulling into a station. Bennell is returning from a medical convention after a call from his nurse. The prologue — the scene in the hospital prior to the train arriving in Santa Mira — was added to the film when the studio wanted the ending changed.

At his office, Bennell finds six cancelled appointments. His time is put to good use, though, when Becky Driscoll (Dana Wynter) appears, an old flame. Becky tells him about her cousin Wilma, who is convinced her Uncle Ira is not Uncle Ira, but some impossible other person, who only looks like Ira. At Wilma's, Miles sits in a swing with her and Becky while Ira mows the lawn. Wilma is desperate as she tries to convince the doctor about what is wrong with Ira. "There's no difference you can actually see. There's something missing. No emotion, no feeling." Miles' voice-over narration lends an urgency to the action as he ruefully says he should have known there was something to the first strange reports. At the Sky Terrace restaurant that evening, he and Becky see two colleagues of Miles' in the parking lot, another doctor, and Dan Kaufman (Larry Gates), a psychiatrist. They tell Miles there is a contagion of the reports of people who aren't themselves. After the doctors drive off, Miles kisses Becky and says, "Mmm. You're Becky Driscoll."

Jack Belicec, a friend of Miles', phones the restaurant and asks him to come over immediately. Jack and his wife Theodora (King Donovan and Carolyn Jones) lead Miles and Becky into a kitchen and den. The scene is photographed from the opposite end of the room. When Miles comes toward a pool table and turns on a low overhead light, the focus sharpens on a sheet. He pulls the sheet back from over a body Jack found in his cellar, a strange, imprecise replica of a man, "Like the first impression of a coin. It isn't finished." It doesn't even look alive enough to be called dead. They ink its fingers and roll five perfectly blank ovals off the fingertips onto a sheet of paper.

Theodora begins to describe the resemblance between the blank body and Jack, and he

Miles finds another of the bodies in a storage bin in the basement.

breaks a glass in his hand listening to her, the cut in his palm drawing blood. The image of the hand in this famous scene was used in advertising artwork for the film; an entire inked handprint appears stamped above the running figures of Miles and Becky. A good deal more imagination went into the appearance of another hand featured in BODY SNATCHERS ads, a drooping claw hand with curved talons that never appears in the movie! This clutching hand came complete with slogans about "Theys" and "The Things" that came from outer space, an extrapolation on customary alien invasions that has nothing to do with the movie.

Miles and Jack decide the body should be watched during the night, and the Belicecs agree to sit up with it. The scene is shot from the position of the body again. And we return to the hand. Jack is asleep at the bar as we see the body's eyes blink and open. All the action in the room draws towards the form on the table; the body and the camera are like a magnet. Theodora frets looking towards the body and walks near it. There is a cut in the palm of a hand now, like Jack's; the wound pulses. Theodora sees the blood and shrieks out. The eyes close as Jack jerks awake. The body is turning into Jack she cries, and the two race to Miles'.

Miles phones Dan Kaufman to join the three of them. He then remembers dropping Becky home, how her father stepped up into the hall from the cellar steps. A horrible intuition grips Miles and he runs out of the house and drives to Becky's, careening up onto the curb in his panic. He hesitates at the door and instead breaks into a small basement window. There in the basement, in a storage bin, he finds another of the bodies, this one turning into Becky. Miles spirits Becky from the house without waking her father. Miles and Jack, with Kaufman, return to Jack's and find the first body gone; when they reconnoiter the basement at Becky's, there is no body. Kaufman tries to reassure the two men. They, too, have become victims of the epidemic of hysteria; what they found was the body of a murdered man. At that point, Nick, a town policeman, sticks his head in the basement window, and Becky's father appears down the stairs. Nick tells them a body with no fingerprints was found in a burning haystack and Jack and Miles quit their protests.

In the morning, Miles is startled by a sound in his basement. He looks down and is relieved to see only Charlie, the gas man. Charlie was played by director Sam Peckinpah in a credited bit part; Peckinpah was Siegel's assistant on the film and is also reputed to have given uncredited help with the screenplay. Downtown, Wilma steps from her shop to tell Miles she's fine now, and asks about Becky. She steps back inside closing the shop, turning to tell Becky's father she is at Miles'. That evening, the two couples are preparing a barbeque when the full horror of the situation is at last made clear. The four

The two couples cower as they step near the impossible sight in the greenhouse.

characters are seen through a greenhouse door. The camera pulls further back into the greenhouse as Miles enters it for some charcoal. The confusion of the foliage inside is exotic and disorienting. Miles starts at a sound and looks down the greenhouse rows.

The scene is another version of the body on the pool table. But now there are four large seed pods, bursting open with bubbly foam oozing around obscured white forms. The two couples cower as they step near the impossible sight: a version of each of them lying tucked under the shelving of the greenhouse. Wisps of the foam blow from one of the bodies; it is Miles. It is the ultimate threat, an alien assumption of one's self. The four are dumbstruck with fright. Miles can only gasp, "Anything is possible. Atomic radiation on plant life or animals." The Belicecs leave for help and Miles returns to the greenhouse. He stabs a pitchfork into the pod bodies, hesitating only a moment before plunging the fork into the form of himself.

In a short time, the scope of the menace is also apparent. At a gas station, a neighborhood serviceman puts two of the pods into the trunk of Miles' car. At his nurse Sally's, Miles sees a number of cars in front and sneaks to a side window to eavesdrop. Sally stands holding a pod to be placed next to her baby's crib. She says, "Now there'll be no more tears." Suddenly Nick, the policeman, takes Miles by the arm and says they've been expecting him. Miles flees across the lawn to the waiting auto. A police radio broadcasts an all points alert for Miles and Becky, but the two manage to hide overnight in Miles' office. The next morning brings the last terrible blows. At 7:45 they see the police meet a Greyhound bus and take arriving passengers off in a car. Then people begin to appear from everywhere, walking towards the small, triangular square in the main intersection. First one truck and then two more arrive, loaded with pods. A policeman begins to call off the names of surrounding communities, and people step forward to take pods. It is the invasion.

The door opens into the office. It is Jack and Kaufman, but they are the new versions. Now the shattering truth is spelled out. Jack and Kaufman try to calm Miles and Becky. They appeal to them to stop fighting; they say it is inevitable. Other men carry in two pods as Kaufman speaks: "Less than a month ago, Santa Mira was like any other town. People with nothing but problems. Then out of the sky came a solution. Seeds drifting through space for years took root in a farmer's field. From the seeds came pods which had the power to reproduce themselves in the exact likeness of any form of life. Your new bodies are growing in there. They're taking you over cell for cell, atom for atom. There's no pain. Suddenly, while you're asleep, they'll absorb your minds, your memories, and you're reborn into an untroubled world. Tomorrow you'll be one of us. There's no need for love. Love, desire, ambition, faith, without them life is so simple, believe me."

People step forward to take the pods. It is the invasion.

The change, the threat from the pods, is an oblivion, an anonymous sameness that enters the people in their unfeeling, uncaring regard of all things. With no emotions, the people become dehumanized and uniform. It is the loss of identity and individuality that is so frightening in the movie, a displacement of the self. It is a psychological doom, but with certain political undertones. The great threatening sameness — however much it results from the pods from space, is not unlike popular notions of the greatest threat of the decade, communism, whereby the individual is regimented into a cipher. This purging of the mind also rang with echoes from the Korean War and reports of brainwashing, sinister regimens that undid soldiers' minds.

Becky and Miles are locked in the office to finally fall asleep from exhaustion. In Finney's novel, one of the eeriest scenes comes when Miles devises sort of voodoo stand-ins for the chameleon pods to imitate. He lays two human skeletons on the floor, sprinkles them with drops of his and Becky's blood, and puts locks of their hair on the skulls. The pods generate two substitute skeletons and Miles' originals dissolve into gray traces. In the movie, Miles settles for knockout syringes he and Becky use to inject and overcome Jack and Kaufman. Then begins one of the most famous and most chilling chase sequences in film.

On the street below, Miles tells Becky they must fake the change and act blankly. But Becky cries out when a truck almost strikes a dog and gives herself away — she is not the affectless twin Becky. The two begin to run up the street as a policeman and more and more townspeople join the chase. Then the air-raid horns are turned on, the great clarions of civil defense. It is like the day the bomb comes, the apocalypse at last. The growing mob fills the small side streets as though the entire town is chasing them. Becky and Miles stagger and fall on concrete steps leading up a hillside. They cross some brush and enter a large cave. Miles loosens some wooden boards and they hide beneath a walkway as the feet of the crowd crash and mill over their heads. The pressed intimacy of the cramped space is like their coffin.

When the crowd passes on, the two splash water in their faces to stay awake in the cave. The pool of water reflects two Beckies, two Miles. They hear an ethereal music and Miles goes to look. He climbs over a rise and finds the master greenhouses, a field of the pods under cultivation. When he returns to the cave, Miles and Becky embrace in a replay of the kiss in the restaurant parking lot. But this time she is not Becky Driscoll. Her glassy expression fills the screen, then Miles' face broken in fearsome recognition. She says, "I went to sleep, Miles, and it happened. They were right." She cries out their hiding place and Miles bolts from the cave.

The mob fills the side streets chasing Miles and Becky.

Here three endings to the story diverge. Finney's novel ends with Miles and Becky together on the hillside. Becky has not changed and Miles sets the field of pods on fire. The crowd of townspeople catch them, but a remarkable thing happens. Out of the gasoline blaze, the remaining pods begin to rise up, more and more of them, until the night sky is dotted with pods quitting the planet. The townspeople watch mutely and then release the couple. Miles reasons the pods somehow realized the extent of human opposition and set sail for a more hospitable planet.

The film's original ending was considerably less optimistic. Miles makes it to the highway in search of people from outside Santa Mira. He climbs aboard a truck but falls back off in shock when he lifts a tarp and finds the truck is loaded with pods. Then he blindly stumbles back into the traffic crying, "You're next! You're next!" His finger points out from the screen to the audience. The film had preview screenings with this ending, and some prints of this version made their way to European theaters. But studio heads became concerned about negative reaction to the sobering conclusion.

When it was clear that someone was going to change the ending to lighten the tone of the climax, Siegel and Wanger added to the film rather than have the ending cut. The prologue and epilogue — the artifice of the frame added to the movie — and Miles' voice-over narration, were the new elements. The traffic scene dissolves back to the hospital from the film's beginning and Miles concludes his story. Then an orderly enters with a remark about a traffic injury, a truck driver: "We had to dig him out from under the most peculiar things I ever saw. They looked like great big seed pods." When the psychiatrist hears that, the alarm is sounded and the world saved. (Kevin McCarthy makes a cameo appearance in the 1978 BODY SNATCHERS — set in San Francisco — playing a running man who cries out, "They're here," as though Miles is still sounding the warning two decades later; director Siegel also appears briefly in the re-make as a cabdriver.)

INVASION OF THE BODY SNATCHERS touched on a serious concern in the 50s, "conformity," the dulling of uniqueness at the beginning of the computer age. Siegel said the film was about a general state of mind really, a gradual vacantness entering American lives. The film was supposed to bring people up short about themselves, what was missing in their lives. In INVASION OF THE BODY SNATCHERS, the future begins in the most pedestrian of present times, with the predicament of people struggling to stay human. Miles says, "Only when we have to fight to stay human do we realize how precious it is." People will make the future what they make of themselves.

Miles stumbles back into the traffic crying, "You're next! You're next!"

FILMOGRAPHY

DESTINATION MOON   1950   Eagle-Lion   Technicolor

Producer: George Pal,   Director: Irving Pichel,   Screenplay: Rip Van Ronkel, Robert A. Heinlein, James O'Hanlon (from the novel, ROCKETSHIP GALILEO, by Robert A. Heinlein),   Art Director: Ernst Fegte,   Astronomical Art: Chesley Bonestell,   Makeup: Webster Philips,   Cinematography: Lionel Lindon,   Special Effects: Lee Zavitz,   Model Animation: John S. Abbott,   Cartoon Animation: Walter Lantz,   Editor: Duke Goldstone, Sound: William Lynch,   Music: Leith Stevens,   Orchestrations: David Tarbet, Technical Advisers: Robert A. Heinlein, Chesley Bonestell.
Cast (role/actor):   Cargraves: Warner Anderson,   Thayer: Tom Powers,   Barnes: John Archer,   Sweeney: Dick Wesson,   Brown: Ted Warde,   Mrs. Cargraves: Erin O'Brien Moore.

THE THING   1951   RKO

Producer: Howard Hawks,   Director: Christian Nyby,   Screenplay: Charles Lederer (from the short story, "Who Goes There?" by John W. Campbell, Jr.),   Art Direction: Albert D'Agostino, John J. Hughes,   Makeup: Lee Greenway,   Cinematography: Russell V. Harlan,   Special Effects Cinematography: Linwood Dunn,   Special Effects: Donald Stewart,   Editor: Roland Gross,   Sound: Phil Brigandi, Clem Portman, Music: Dimitri Tiomkin.
Cast (role/actor):   Hendry: Kenneth Tobey,   Nikki: Margaret Sheridan,   Scotty: Douglas Spencer,   Carrington: Robert Cornthwaite,   Thing: James Arness,   Dykes: James Young,   Bob: Dewey Martin,   Mac: Robert Nichols,   Vorrhees: Paul Frees,   Fogerty: David McMann,   Redding: George Fennemen,   Fred: Robert Stevenson.

THE DAY THE EARTH STOOD STILL   1951   20th Century Fox

Producer: Julian Blaustein,   Director: Robert Wise,   Screenplay: Edmund H. North (from the short story, "Farewell to the Master," by Harry Bates),   Art Direction: Lyle Wheeler, Addison Hehr,   Cinematography: Leo Tover,   Special Effects: Fred Sersen,   Editor: William Reynolds,   Music: Bernard Hermann,   Technical Adviser: Dr. Samuel Herrick.
Cast (role/actor):   Klaatu: Michael Rennie,   Helen: Patricia Neal,   Bobby: Billy Gray, Barnhardt: Sam Jaffee,   Stevens: Hugh Marlowe,   Gort: Lock Martin. Also: Francis Bavier, James Seay,   Frank Conroy,   Carleton Young,   Drew Pearson,   H.V. Kaltenborn.

WHEN WORLDS COLLIDE   1951   Paramount   Technicolor

Producer: George Pal,   Director: Rudolph Maté,   Screenplay: Sydney Boehm (from the novel, WHEN WORLDS COLLIDE, by Edwin Balmer and Philip Wylie),   Art Direction: Hal Pereira,   Al Nozaki,   Astronomical Art, Technical Adviser: Chesley Bonestell,   Makeup: Wally Westmore,   Cinematography: John F. Seitz, W. Howard Greene,   Process Cinematography: Farciot Edouart,   Special Effects: Gordon Jennings, Harry Barndollar,   Editors: Arthur Schmidt, Doane Harrison,   Sound: Walter Oberst, Music: Leith Stevens.
Cast (role/actor):   Randall: Richard Derr,   Joyce: Barbara Rush,   Stanton: John Hoyt,   Hendron: Larry Keating,   Drake: Peter Hanson,   Frey: Stephen Chase, Bronson: Hayden Rorke,   Ferris: Frank Cady,   Julie: Judith Ames,   Announcer: Paul Frees, Ottinger: Sandro Giglio,   Stewardess: Laura Elliott.

IT CAME FROM OUTER SPACE   1953   Universal   3-D

Producer: William Alland,   Director: Jack Arnold,   Screenplay: Harry Essex,   Story: Ray Bradbury,   Art Direction: Bernard Herzbrun, Robert Boyle,   Makeup and design: Bud Westmore, Milicent Patrick,   Cinematography: Clifford Stine,   Special Effects Cinematography: Stanley Horsley,   Editor: Paul Weatherwax,   Sound: Leslie I. Carey, Glenn Anderson,   Music: Herman Stein,   Musical Director: Joseph Gershenson.
Cast (role/actor):   Putnam: Richard Carlson,   Ellen: Barbara Rush,   Sheriff: Charles Drake,   George: Russell Johnson,   Frank: Joe Sawyer. Also: Kathleen Hughes,   Alan Dexter,   Dave Willock,   George Eldridge,   Morey Amsterdam.

INVADERS FROM MARS   1953   20th Century Fox   Cinecolor

Producer: Edward L. Alperson, Sr.,   Director and Design: William Cameron Menzies, Screenplay: Richard Blake, John Tucker Battle, William Cameron Menzies,   Story: John Tucker Battle,   Art Director: Boris Leven,   Makeup: Gene Hibbs, Steve Dunn, Cinematography: John F. Seitz,   Special Effects: Jack Cosgrove, Theodore Lydecker, Irving Block, Jack Rabin,   Editor: Arthur Roberts,   Sound: Earl Crane, Sr.,   Music: Raoul Kraushaar,   Additional Sequences Director: Wesley Barry.
Cast (role/actor):   David MacLean: Jimmy Hunt,   Pat: Helena Carter,   Kelston: Arthur Franz, Fielding: Morris Ankrum,   MacLean: Leif Erickson,   Mrs. MacLean: Hillary Brooke, Rinaldi: Max Wagner,   Roth: Milburn Stone,   Finley: Walter Sande,   Intelligence: Luce Potter,   Mutants: Max Palmer, Lock Martin.

WAR OF THE WORLDS 1953 Paramount Technicolor

Producer: George Pal, Director: Byron Haskin, Screenplay: Barré Lyndon (from the novel, WAR OF THE WORLDS, by H. G. Wells), Art Direction: Al Nozaki, Hal Pereira, Astronomical Art: Chesley Bonestell, Makeup: Wally Westmore, Cinematography: George Barnes, Special Effects: Gordon Jennings, Wallace Kelley, Paul Lerpal, Ivyl Burks, Jan Demila, Irmin Roberts, Walter Hoffman, Editor: Everett Douglas, Sound: Gene Garvin, Walter Oberst, Don Johnson, Harry Lindgren, Music: Leith Stevens, Technical Adviser: Dr. Robert Richardson.
Cast (role/actor): Forrester: Gene Barry, Sylvia: Ann Robinson, Mann: Les Tremayne, Collins: Lewis Martin, Pryor: Robert Cornthwaite, Bilderbeck: Sandro Giglio, Announcer: Paul Frees, Narrator: Sir Cedric Hardwicke, Martian: Charles Gemora, Hefner: Vernon Rich, Salvatore: Jack Kruschen, Hogue: Paul Birch, Perry: Bill Phipps.

BEAST FROM 20,000 FATHOMS 1953 Warner Bros.

Producers: Hal Chester, Jack Dietz, Director: Eugene Lourie, Screenplay: Lou Morheim, Fred Freiberger (from the short story, "The Foghorn," by Ray Bradbury), Art Director: Hall Waller, Makeup: Louis Phillippi, Cinematography: Jack Russell, Technical Effects: Ray Harryhausen, Special Effects: Willis Cook, Editors: Bernard W. Burton, Clarence Kolster, Sound: Max Hutchinson, Music: David Buttolph, Orchestrations: Maurice de Packh.
Cast (role/actor): Nesbitt: Paul Christian, Leigh: Paula Raymond, Elson: Cecil Kellaway, Evans: Kenneth Tobey, Stone: Lee Van Cleef, Loomis: Steve Brodie, Ingersoll: King Donovon, Jackson: Donald Woods, Jacob: Jack Pennick, Ritchie: Ross Elliott, Morton: Frank Ferguson.

THEM 1954 Warner Bros.

Producer: David Weisbart, Director: Gordon Douglas, Screenplay: Ted Sherdeman, Story: George Worthing Yates, Adaptation: Russell Hughes, Art Director: Stanley Fleischer, Makeup: Gordon Blau, Cinematography: Sid Hickox, Special Effects: Ralph Ayres, Prop Construction: Dick Smith, Editor: Thomas Reilly, Sound: William Mueller, Francis J. Scheid, Music: Bronislau Kaper, Orchestrations: Robert Franklyn.
Cast (role/actor): Petersen: James Whitmore, Pat: Joan Weldon, Medford: Edmund Gwenn, Graham: James Arness, O'Brien: Onslow Stevens, Blackburn: Chris Drake, Little Girl: Sandy Descher, Crotty: Fess Parker, Drunk: Olin Howlin, Sergeant: Leonard Nimoy, Mrs. Lodge: Mary Ann Hokanson, Kibbee: Sean McClory.

CREATURE FROM THE BLACK LAGOON   1954   Universal   3-D

Producer: William Alland,   Director: Jack Arnold,   Screenplay: Harry Essex, Arthur Ross,   Story: Maurice Zimm,   Art Direction: Bernard Herzbrun, Hilyard Brown,   Makeup and design: Bud Westmore, Milicent Patrick, Jack Kevan, Chris Mueller,   Cinematography: William E. Snyder,   Special Effects: Charles S. Welbourne,   Editor: Ted J. Kent,   Musical Director: Joseph Gershenson.
Cast (role/actor):   Reed: Richard Carlson,   Katy: Julia Adams,   Williams: Richard Denning,   Lucas: Nestor Paiva,   Maia: Antonio Moreno,   Creature: Ricou Browning,   Ben Chapman.   Also: Whit Bissell,   Rodd Redwing,   Julio Lopez.

IT CAME FROM BENEATH THE SEA   1955   Columbia

Producer: Charles H. Schneer,   Executive Producer: Sam Katzman,   Director: Robert Gordon,   Screenplay: George Worthing Yates, Hal Smith,   Story: George Worthing Yates,   Art Director: Paul Palmentola,   Cinematography: Henry Freulich,   Technical Effects: Ray Harryhausen,   Special Effects: Jack Erickson,   Editor: Jerome Thoms,   Sound: Josh Westmoreland,   Music: Mischa Bakaleinikoff.
Cast (role/actor):   Mathews: Kenneth Tobey,   Lesley: Faith Domergue,   Carter: Donald Curtis,   Burns: Ian Keith,   Nash: Harry Lauter,   Stacy: Richard Peterson,   Norman: Dean Maddox, Jr.,   Chase: Del Courtney,   McLoed: Ed Fisher,   Griff: Chuck Griffiths.

THIS ISLAND EARTH   1955   Universal   Technicolor

Producer: William Alland,   Director: Joseph Newman,   Screenplay: Franklin Coen, Edward G. O'Callaghan (from the novel, THIS ISLAND EARTH, by Raymond F. Jones),   Art Direction: Alexander Golitzen, Richard H. Riedel,   Makeup and design: Bud Westmore, Milicent Patrick, Jack Kevan, Chris Mueller, Robert Hickman,   Cinematography: Clifford Stine,   Special Effects Cinematography: Clifford Stine, Stanley Horsley,   Special Effects: Charles Baker,   Editor: Virgil Vogel,   Music: Herman Stein,   Musical Director: Joseph Gershenson.
Cast (role/actor):   Exeter: Jeff Morrow,   Ruth: Faith Domergue,   Meachum: Rex Reason,   Brack: Lance Fuller,   Carlton: Russell Johnson,   Wilson: Robert Nichols,   Monitor: Douglas Spencer,   Mutant: Eddie Parker,   Engelborger: Karl Lindt.   Also: Regis Barton, Bart Roberts.

FORBIDDEN PLANET   1956   MGM   Eastmancolor   Cinemascope

Producer: Nicholas Nayfack,   Director: Fred M. Wilcox,   Screenplay: Cyril Hume,   Story: Irving Block, Allen Adler,   Art Direction: Arthur Lonergan, Cedric Gibbons, Irving Block, Makeup: William Tuttle,   Cinematography: George J. Folsey,   Special Effects: A. Arnold Gillespie, Warren Newcombe, Irving G. Ries, Joshua Meador, Matthew Yuricich,   Editor: Ferris Webster,   Sound: Wesley C. Miller,   Electronic Tonalities: Louis and Bebe Barron.
Cast (role / actor): Morbius: Walter Pidgeon,   Altaira: Anne Francis,   Adams: Leslie Nielsen,   Ostrow: Warren Stevens,   Farman: Jack Kelly,   Quinn: Richard Anderson, Cook: Earl Holliman,   Bosun: George Wallace,   Robby: Frank Carpenter,   Frank Darrow. Also: James Drury,   Bob Dix.

INVASION OF THE BODY SNATCHERS   Allied Artists   1956

Producer: Walter Wanger,   Director: Don Siegal,   Screenplay: Daniel Mainwaring (from the novel, THE BODY SNATCHERS, by Jack Finney),   Art Director: Edward Haworth, Makeup: Emile LaVigne,   Cinematography: Ellsworth Fredricks,   Special Effects: Milt Rice,   Editor: Robert S. Eisen,   Sound: Ralph Butler, Del Harris, Music: Carmen Dragon.
Cast (role / actor): Bennell: Kevin McCarthy,   Becky: Dana Wynter,   Belicec: King Donovon, Theodora: Carolyn Jones,   Kaufman: Larry Gates,   Wilma: Virginia Christie,   Ira: Tom Fadden,   Sally: Jean Willes,   Nick: Ralph Dumke,   Hill: Whit Bissell,   Doctor: Richard Deacon,   Charlie: Sam Peckinpah.

AFTERWORD

The decade didn't end in 1956. Neither did the wave of sci-fi movies subside. If anything, science fiction avidness grew in the culture, beyond the Hollywood pale. COLLIER'S magazine ran an influential and prophetic two-year series of articles on man in space. Space Cadet books, lunchboxes, and milk mugs appeared. On the radio there was SPACE PATROL. On TV, CAPTAIN VIDEO, SCIENCE FICTION THEATER, and a highly regarded three-part space series on Walt Disney's show. But something happened in 1957 that changed the way people looked at space flight, and the very nature of science fiction. A newspaper headline from October that year put it simply: "Science Fiction Becomes Fact." And a radio announcer dramatically harkened to his audience, "Listen now, for the sound which forever separates the old from the new . . . ." — the faint, distant beeping of the orbiting Russian space satellite, Sputnik.

The Russian feat — on October 4, 1957 — sent convulsions through the U.S. There was, indeed, a space race on. Rudely spurred, the U.S. space program was able to put a satellite in orbit in January 1958. A billion dollars was quickly coughed up by Congress for the National Defense Education Act, to try and buy the country more education and more brainpower. Science fiction and the specific future of space flight became serious business. An innocence went out of things, and the disenchanting spell of facts entered in. Still, the past is intact. Back around the corner, the other side of 1957, these films remain, defining an era that was complete and entire in its general terms by 1956, and never again the same after 1957.

Working on this book I traveled in time, back to years downtown in the 50s. The experience was like trying to recreate the past, and see how much of it would return. Seeing the films again in a short, concentrated period of time was a re-emersion in that world, Hardy's Theater again, and a Saturday afternoon crowd of children that erupted into a relieved cheer when the psychiatrist says call the F.B.I. at the end of INVASION OF THE BODY SNATCHERS. I watched with fascination as my two young children first saw the films, screening them in our home. When we would see a film, I would sit with a pile of pictures and watch for the wonderful moment when the picture appeared in the screen action, like a photographic image appearing out of the blur of a developing tray. My search for materials turned up rare photos that occasionally bore 25 years' wear, but which captured extraordinary scenes.

INVASION OF THE BODY SNATCHERS: The master greenhouses, a field of the pods under cultivation.

The adventure led to Hollywood and the home of Forrest J. ("Forry") Ackerman, known as "Mr. Science Fiction," the world's greatest fan of sci-fi/horror/fantasy, with the largest collection anywhere of memorabilia, originals, artifacts, and more than 100,000 photographs from the movies. The morning of my first visit there the sun shone its Hollywood hills brightness on the red Cadillac in front, and its license plate, "SCI FI." Forry was an affable host, and expansively shared with me marvels like the miniature Golden Gate Bridge from IT CAME FROM BENEATH THE SEA, the single remaining Martian war craft from WAR OF THE WORLDS, James Arness' claw hands from THE THING, one of the original costume heads from CREATURE FROM THE BLACK LAGOON. Forry is the twenty-year editor of FAMOUS MONSTERS OF FILMLAND magazine and a literary agent; he sold THIS ISLAND EARTH to the movies. The two rings he wears were gifts from Boris Karloff and Bela Lugosi, from their roles in THE MUMMY and DRACULA; Forry has one of Lugosi's three Dracula capes. In a small case I saw Fritz Lang's monocle.

During one of our visits, I asked Forry about locations of scenes in INVASION OF THE BODY SNATCHERS, and the stairs up the hillside. He said he didn't recall any stairs, but gave me directions to a nearby Hollywood neighborhood, up one of the canyons, where I would see some familiar sights. Sure enough, it was a side street from the chase sequence. Driving around the area, I suddenly saw a metal railing barely noticeable at the side of a street. There, like a secret, was the stairway up the hillside, tucked between two obviously new homes — built since the late 50s — and obscured even further in wild foliage. This piece of science fiction had stood still in time.

Some time later I made my way to the second location I was looking for, the curious triangular square where the trucks unload the pods. In the small town of Sierra Madre, just east of Pasadena, was Kersting Court, the setting in the film. I was walking around the three sides of the small grassy area and trees, gratified. Suddenly, the air horn blasted — the one signaling the start of the chase. I was stunned. The intersection continued its busy commotion after the single piercing sound. I eventually got to a tiny newspaper office and was told the fire horn is sounded daily to test it. Every day for 23 years. I was amazed. As the sun — the clock on the wall — tips on overhead into yet another decade, the great air horn still resounds daily — once at noon — in Sierra Madre.

DS

Return to BODY SNATCHERS land: the author at the stairway up the hillside.

DENNIS SALEH was born in Chicago and raised in Fresno, California. He was educated in California and Arizona, and has lectured for the University of California and California State University. He is the author of four books of poetry and editor of an anthology of contemporary American poetry. Saleh lives on the Monterey Peninsula in California, with his wife and two children, and is editor and publisher of Comma Books.